"But who do you say that I am?"

By
William Stewart Whittemore

*"He said to them, "But who do you say that I am?"
Peter answered and said, "The Christ of God."
Luke 9:20*

Copyright © 2009 by William Stewart Whittemore

"But who do you say that I am?"
by William Stewart Whittemore

Printed in the United States of America

ISBN 9781607919490

All rights reserved solely by the author. The author guaran-tees all contents are original and do not infringe upon the legal rights of any other person or work. No part of this book may be reproduced in any form without the permission of the author. The views expressed in this book are not necessarily those of the publisher.

Unless otherwise indicated, Bible quotations are taken from
The Holy Bible, New King James Version. Copyright
© 1982 by Thomas Nelson, Inc., Used by permis-sion. Biblesoft software used.
Josephus The Complete Works, translated by William
Whiston, A.M. Copyright © 1998 by Thomas Nelson
Publishers.

www.xulonpress.com

Dedicated to Jesus Christ
For
His Glory and Praise

Acknowledgements

First and foremost, I thank the Dear Holy Spirit for the inspiration to write this book. And for His counsel and revelations in preparing this manuscript for the glory of our Dear Holy Father in Heaven and for the lifting up of our Dear Lord and Savior, Jesus Christ. It was only by His gracious responses to my requests for understanding, which He provided through His Holy Word, other people and the circumstances in my life that He took me through, that this book could ever have been written. Toda Roba L'El!!!

My loving appreciation also goes out to all in my dear family who took back their prodigal dad and relative. And being next door to my dear daughter Suzette, and her wonderful family, I am blessed to continually experience their love and support.

And many thanks go out to, Bette Jo Martinoli, Chaplain Sandi Richard and Patrick Harbison. They all provided much needed suggestions and editing corrections, which only enhanced this labor of love.

Contents

Introduction xi

Part I	The Great I AM 15
Chapter One	The Road to Emmaus 17
Chapter Two	The Angel of The LORD 21
Chapter Three	LORD of Hosts 31
Chapter Four	Son of Man 47
Chapter Five	Melchizedek 55
Chapter Six	Son of God 59
Part II	Messianic Prophesies 73
Chapter Seven	The Seed of God 75
Chapter Eight	Messiah's Birth and Mission 95
Chapter Nine	Our Messiah and His Miracles 107

"But who do you say that I am?"

Chapter Ten   Messiah's Passion and Triumph.........115

Chapter Eleven   Messiah's Glory 129

Chapter Twelve Revelation 155

Introduction

❧ ☙

After nearly three and one half years with His disciples Jesus asked them the most important question of their lives: "But who do you say that I am?" How would we answer Jesus if He asked that question of us today? Could we proclaim from the heart like Peter, *"The Christ of God!"* Jesus, the Christ, the manifestation of Almighty God in the flesh of man.

Before posing that question to His disciples, Jesus prepared them with His teachings from the Hebrew Scriptures.

The Hebrew Scriptures are known today as the "Tanach," or the "Old Testament," as most Christians are familiar. The word **Tanach** is comprised of <u>letters</u> in Hebrew that represent the three sections of the Hebrew Bible:

1. **T**or**a**h-The Law
2. **Na**viim-The Prophets
3. **K**tiviot-The Writings (The "K" in this word is pronounced as the Hebrew letter "Chaf" or "**ch**")

Torah, the Law, is comprised of the first five books of the Tanach (Genesis through Deuteronomy). This organization is the same in all Christian Bibles, but this is the only

"But who do you say that I am?"

section that corresponds to the organization of the Christian Old Testament.

Naviim, the Prophets, comprises what is known today as the Major and Minor Prophets (Samuel, Isaiah, Malachi, for example), but excluding Daniel.

Ktiviot, the Writings, includes the Books of Ruth, Esther and Psalms, for example, and ending with the Books of First and Second Chronicles.

What is interesting about this organization of the Bible is that Jesus referred to this system for the Hebrew Bible hundreds of years before the rabbis actually organized the Tanach in this way. We can see this in Luke 24:44 when Jesus said;

*"These are the words which I spoke to you while I was still with you, that all things must be fulfilled which were written in the **Law** of Moses and the **Prophets** and the **Psalms** concerning Me."*

Where is all this leading? It is important for us to see Jesus in the Tanach (Old Testament) as well as the New Testament for two main reasons.

First, on the road to Emmaus when Jesus walked with the two disciples on the day He was raised from the dead, they did not recognize their Savior. Therefore, He patiently explained to them in detail what the Tanach said about Him.

"And beginning at Moses and all the Prophets, He expounded to them in all the Scriptures the things concerning Himself" (Luke 24:27). Why did He do this? Because as He said, *"O foolish ones, and*

"But who do you say that I am?"

slow of heart to believe *in all that the prophets have spoken! Ought not the Christ to have suffered these things and to enter into His glory?"* (Luke 24:25-26-Emphasis added).

The passages that Jesus explained to them were from the Old Testament. At this time, the New Testament had not yet been written. If we are to fully understand God's redemptive plan for us and to know Jesus more fully, we too must "seek His face" in the Old Testament.

Second, if we are to truly know Jesus, not just know about Him, we must let God reveal Himself to us through all of Scripture. As Jesus explained to us in John 17:3, *"And this is eternal life, that they may know You, the only true God, and Jesus Christ whom You have sent"* ("The Word made flesh"). Furthermore, we are told how vital the Word of God should be in our lives, as well as in the lives of Jesus' disciples;

"All Scripture is given by inspiration of God, and is profitable for doctrine, for reproof, for correction, for instruction in righteousness, that the man of God may be complete, thoroughly equipped for every good work." (2 Timothy 3:16-17).

How can we get started on this journey and know "the only true God and Jesus Christ?" Jesus again tells us in Luke 24:25 when He spoke further to His two disciples, *"in all Scripture the things concerning Himself."* In other words, by letting our Father by the Holy Spirit reveal Jesus fully to us. It is then we can answer as Peter had done without any doubt, Jesus is "The Christ of God!"

It is my hope and prayer that this book will instill a desire in your heart to search all the Bible for yourself and see the face of Jesus more clearly than you ever have before.

"But who do you say that I am?"

For this quest, in Part I of this book, we will travel on the Road to Emmaus and "listen" in on what Jesus might have taught His disciples on that beautiful Resurrection Day. Then, in Part II, we will look at some of the many prophesies written about Jesus, our Messiah, in the Old Testament (The Tanach) and see their fulfillment as recorded in the New Testament. We will also look at those unfulfilled prophesies concerning the return of our Savior. Finally, we will see Jesus revealed to His traveling companions when they stopped to eat after that wonderful walk together and witness Jesus "break bread" for them.

"Did not our heart burn within us while He talked with us on the road, and while He opened the Scriptures to us?" (Luke 24:32).

Halleluyah!!!

PART I

THE GREAT I AM

CHAPTER ONE

The Road To Emmaus

֎֎ ֎֎

Luke 24:27
And beginning at Moses and all the Prophets,
He expounded to them in all the Scriptures
the things concerning Himself.

"What things?" This is what Jesus said to His two disciples on the road to Emmaus on the day of His Resurrection (Luke 24:13-35). They were astonished that this "Stranger" did not know what had happened in Jerusalem these last few days. They didn't recognize Him as their risen Savior. And, in answering Jesus they said, *"The things concerning Jesus of Nazareth, who was a Prophet mighty in deed and word before God and all the people, and how the chief priests and our rulers delivered Him to be condemned to death, and crucified Him."* (Luke 24:19-20). Jesus' question was intended to open their eyes to who He really was, not only their Savior but the "Great I Am." Jesus then took them on a journey through the Hebrew Scriptures (Old Testament); *"And beginning at Moses and all the Prophets, He expounded to them in all the Scriptures the things concerning Himself"* (Luke 24:27).

"But who do you say that I am?"

"What things?" This question could be asked of us today as we wait and look for our returning Savior on our "road to Emmaus." Not too many church attendees today would recognize our Jewish Messiah, since most of the teachings about Him are from the New Testament. Those teachings are not wrong, but to fully know Jesus, the Living Word of God, we need to know him by the Holy Spirit and all of God's Word. Just as those disciples did not recognize Him until Jesus revealed Himself in His Word and then broke bread with them, I too am convinced we will not deeply know Jesus without our seeing Him, personally, not only in the New Testament, but also in the Old Testament.

Therefore, the purpose of this book is to help us see and know Jesus in a more personal and in a much deeper way. I am hopeful that you will see Jesus the Christ clearly as the One who said of Himself, *"before Abraham was, I AM"* *(John 8:58b)*, *"— the God of Abraham, the God of Isaac, and the God of Jacob..."* (Exodus 3:6).

While reading this intriguing account of Jesus and His disciples in Luke 24:13-35 my question has been, "What Scriptures did Jesus expound on?" Oh yes, there are some obvious verses one could point to, for example, Isaiah 7:14; 9:6-7; 53, to name just a fraction of what the Old Testament reveals about Jesus. But what special verses, passages and chapters did Jesus choose to share with His disciples? How long did Jesus spend explaining the Scriptures that pointed to Him? One can only guess and surmise.

We can, however, come up with some pretty good assumptions from this Emmaus walk with the Lord as told in this passage of Luke. For example,

- We are told the walk from Jerusalem to Emmaus was seven miles long. Now let's assume Jesus met up with His disciples, Cleopus and his companion, right

"But who do you say that I am?"

at the beginning of their walk. This would indicate Jesus was with them at least 3 ½ hours.

- Jesus could have covered many verses during that time but the Bible says He expounded on them. This would also seem to indicate that Jesus took His time to explain their meaning. Therefore, one might conclude that Jesus spent considerable time on some very key areas explaining these Scriptures that pointed to Him.

Based on these assumptions and what Jesus and others said in the New Testament, let us look now at some key areas Jesus might have covered about Himself with His two disciples on the road to Emmaus during that glorious Resurrection Day.

We know, for example, God manifested Himself in physical form before the time of the Son of man. One can see God in at least three forms of the pre-incarnate Christ who appeared in the Old Testament. First, and probably the most obvious way the pre-incarnate Jesus appeared was in the form of the Angel of the LORD (the subject of our next chapter). Second, He also appeared to us as Melchizedek, the Lord of Salem (Jerusalem). Third, Jesus is referred to as "The LORD of hosts." There are other ways Jesus is revealed to us in the Hebrew Scriptures (Tanach), and we will also look at those symbolic metaphors later on in this book. But first, let us meet "The Angel of the LORD."

CHAPTER TWO

THE ANGEL OF THE LORD

Exodus 3:2
And the Angel of the LORD appeared to him in
a flame of fire from the midst of a bush. So he
(Moses) looked, and behold, the bush was burning
with fire, but the bush was not consumed.

There are some fifty seven references to "the Angel of the LORD" in the Bible (NKJV). The verse above gives us a direct connection to Jesus because when Moses turned to investigate the burning bush, he then saw the Angel of the LORD. We know this is God because in verse 4 it says, *"God called him from the midst of the bush and said,* *"Moses. Moses."* Then in verse 5 God declares, *"Do not draw near this place. Take your sandals off your feet, for the place where you stand is holy ground."*

How do we know this is the manifestation of pre-incarnate Jesus?" We know this by how God identifies Himself to Moses when, in verse 13 Moses asks God for His name. God's answer is found in verse 14:

"I AM WHO I AM.' And He said, 'Thus you shall say to the children of Israel, 'I AM has sent me to you.'"

21

"But who do you say that I am?"

Now let us look in John 8:58 at what Jesus said about Himself to His brethren. *"Most assuredly, I say to you, before Abraham was, I AM."* Jesus clearly tells us He is not only the Angel of the LORD who spoke to Moses in the burning bush, but He is the manifestation of the Great "I AM."

Before this, we can see that Jesus appeared before Abraham to make His covenant with Abraham and his seed:

"When Abram was ninety-nine years old, the LORD ***appeared*** *to Abram and said to him, 'I am Almighty God; walk before Me and be blameless. And I will make My covenant between Me and you, and will multiply you exceedingly"* (Gen 17:1-2-emphasis added).

Again we see Jesus as the great "I Am," when He appeared to Samson's parents, Manoah and his wife, in the Book of Judges, Chapter 13, as "the Angel of the LORD." This was during the time when Israel was being oppressed by the Philistines because of the evil they had committed against the LORD. But God, in His mercy, was already setting the plan in motion for a Nazirite to be born that would deliver His people from their enemy, the Philistines. Certainly this story is a shadow of things to come when God would send Jesus the Christ to redeem the whole World from our evil and our fiercest enemy, Satan, the devil.

Now in this story Manoah's wife was barren, but the Angel of the LORD appeared to her and told her she would conceive and bear a son who would *"deliver Israel out of the hands of the Philistines."* Manoah's wife then told her husband about her encounter with the *"Man of God"* who had a countenance like *"the Angel of God, very Awesome."* It was after that encounter that *"...Manoah prayed to the LORD, and said, "O my Lord, please let the Man of God*

22

"But who do you say that I am?"

whom You sent come to us again and teach us what we shall do for the child who will be born" (Judges 13:8).

God answered his prayer by reappearing to Manoah's wife. She then rushed to tell her husband, *"Look, the Man who came to me the other day has just now appeared to me!"* (Judges 13:10)

> *"So Manoah arose and followed his wife. When he came to the Man, he said to Him, "Are You the Man who spoke to this woman?" And He said, "I am." Manoah said, "Now let Your words come to pass! What will be the boy's rule of life, and his work?"*
>
> *So the Angel of the LORD said to Manoah, "Of all that I said to the woman let her be careful. She may not eat anything that comes from the vine, nor may she drink wine or similar drink, nor eat anything unclean. All that I commanded her let her observe."*
>
> *Then Manoah said to the Angel of the LORD, "Please let us detain You, and we will prepare a young goat for You." And the Angel of the LORD said to Manoah, "Though you detain Me, I will not eat your food. But if you offer a burnt offering, you must offer it to the LORD." (For Manoah did not know He was the Angel of the LORD.)*
>
> *Then Manoah said to the Angel of the LORD, "What is Your name, that when Your words come to pass we may honor You?" And the Angel of the LORD said to him, "Why do you ask My name, seeing it is wonderful?"'* (Judges 13:11-18)

In answering Manoah, the Angel of the LORD tells him His name; *"it is wonderful."* The word used for wonderful in Hebrew here (paliy, pronounced palee) is from the same root

23

"But who do you say that I am?"

word that forms the word "Wonderful" in Isaiah 9:6 when Isaiah prophesied about the names of Jesus.

Now Manoah realizes he is in the presence of God. *"So Manoah took the young goat with the grain offering, and offered it upon the rock to the LORD. And He did a wondrous thing while Manoah and his wife looked on — it happened as the flame went up toward heaven from the altar — the Angel of the LORD ascended in the flame of the altar! When Manoah and his wife saw this, they fell on their faces to the ground.*

> *When the Angel of the LORD appeared no more to Manoah and his wife, then Manoah knew that He was the Angel of the LORD. And Manoah said to his wife, "We shall surely die, because we have seen God!" But his wife said to him, "If the LORD had desired to kill us, He would not have accepted a burnt offering and a grain offering from our hands, nor would He have shown us all these things, nor would He have told us such things as these at this time."*
>
> *So the woman bore a son and called his name Samson; and the child grew, and the LORD blessed him. And the Spirit of the LORD began to move upon him at Mahaneh Dan between Zorah and Eshtaol"* (Judges 13:19-25).

We can certainly see from this account that the Angel of the LORD is God and yet another manifestation of the pre-incarnate Christ, our Messiah Jesus.

However, one of the most powerful testimonies about The Angel of the LORD is revealed in the story of Abraham's sacrifice of his son Isaac. In this story, in Genesis 22, He shows us He is the pre-incarnate Jesus our Savior and the

"But who do you say that I am?"

suffering servant who gave His life for us in a most powerful way.

How could I ever forget how God personally revealed this mystery to me when one day while reading about Jesus' triumphant entry into Jerusalem (John 12:12-19), I asked the Lord, "Why did You ride into Jerusalem on a donkey?" I knew that Zachariah's prophecy said,

"Rejoice greatly, O daughter of Zion! Shout, O daughter of Jerusalem! Behold, your King is coming to you; He is just and having salvation, Lowly and riding on a donkey, A colt, the foal of a donkey" (Zech 9:9).

Still, even knowing about this prophesy, why a donkey? One could imagine our King on a white stead, or maybe even being carried on the shoulders of His apostles while making that triumphant entrance into Jerusalem. Again, why a donkey?

Then about a year later after asking that question of the Lord, I was reading in Josephus' "Antiquity of the Jews" his commentary on the sacrifice of Isaac by Abraham, it was at that moment the Holy Spirit gave me the answer to my question. As I was reading Josephus' commentary on Genesis 22, I came upon this sentence that quickened my spirit. Josephus stated that when Abraham loaded his donkey for the trip to Mt. Moriah that day, that he (Abraham) put everything needed for the sacrifice upon the donkey.

It was then that I realized Abraham did not have everything on the donkey needed for **The Sacrifice**; Jesus was not, yet, on that donkey! This caused me to go back and read again this wonderful account of Isaac and Abraham in Genesis 22. When I did this I could begin to see even more references to Jesus and His passion for us than I had ever seen before. It was as if Jesus came alive through Isaac. To

25

me I saw clearly for the first time the prophetic message in this passage of His suffering and death on the cross for us.

In remembering this beautiful story of faith and obedience we see how Abraham was commanded by God to take his son Isaac, "his only son," and go to a place that God would show him where he would sacrifice Isaac to God. Abraham at the age of 100 years old had finally fathered his only son with his wife Sarah. One can only imagine how Abraham must have struggled with this command to sacrifice his son.

However, we do get an early glimpse of Abraham's faith and trust in God when in verse 8 we read Abraham's response to Isaac's question in verse 7.

> "*My father!*' Abraham answered, '*Here I am, my son.*' Then Isaac said, '*Look, the fire and the wood, but where is the lamb for a burnt offering?*' Abraham then answered, '*My son, God will provide for Himself the lamb for a burnt offering.*' '*So the two of them went together.*'"

When one looks at the Hebrew language version of this verse there is no preposition "for" before the word "Himself." I believe this verse could say, "God will provide Himself, the Lamb, as (for) the burnt offering."

Jesus referred directly to Abraham's prophetic response to his son when He said in John 8:56, "*Your father Abraham rejoiced to see My day, and he saw it and was glad.*" It must have been something that Abraham had known all along, because of his steadfast faith and trust in God. He knew somehow God was going to restore his son to him even if he had to make a sacrifice of him as God had commanded him to do.

Now in reading the rest of Genesis 22 we can see other parallels to Jesus' triumphal sacrifice on Calvary in our

"But who do you say that I am?"

behalf. For example, starting in verse 3 we see that Abraham took two servants with him, but they were left behind (verse 5) while Abraham and Isaac went up to the mountain for the sacrifice. The parallel here, I believe, is the reference to John and Peter who were the only disciples to follow Jesus to His trial. Also in verse 3 we see the reference to Abraham loading His donkey for the trip. And as I stated earlier this is where Josephus commented that Abraham had put all that was needed for the sacrifice on the donkey. But as the Lord revealed to me, He (Jesus) was not on that donkey. All that was needed for **The Sacrifice** would be when Jesus rode the donkey triumphantly into Jerusalem some four thousand years later.

As many times as I have read this passage I had failed to recognize the significance of the statement in verse 6a where the Bible says, *"So Abraham took the wood of the burnt offering and laid it on Isaac his son."* Now I recognize this verse as referring to the cross being born by Jesus (John 17:1). Also in verse 9b we see another reference to Jesus and the cross when the Bible says, *"He bound his son Isaac and laid him on the altar, **on top of the wood**"* (NIV-emphasis added), this time referring to Jesus being "bound" to the cross for crucifixion (John 17:18).

As an aside, this last observation came to me through a brother, in Christ, who pointed this out to me when I was sharing this revelation with him. I mention this because we all have insights given to us by the Holy Spirit, God's Word, the Bible, and through wonderful brothers and sisters in the Lord. We need to share these revelations with each other for the encouragement and the edification of the Body of Christ.

Now as we continue, just as Abraham stretched out his hand to slay his son Isaac, *"**the Angel of the LORD** called to him from heaven and said, "Abraham, Abraham!"* ... *"Do not lay your hand on the lad, or do anything to him; for*

"But who do you say that I am?"

*now I know that you fear God, since you have not withheld your son, **your only son**, from Me"* (Gen 22:11-12-emphasis added).

Here we can see the pre-incarnate Jesus (the Angel of the LORD), the One who was actually our substitute offering, preventing Abraham from sacrificing his son. But not only that, we see Jesus clearly identifying Himself as God by His statement, *"for now I know that you fear **God**, since you have not withheld your son, your only son, from **Me**"* (emphasis added). In Abraham's ultimate test of faith we see God showing us that when we trust Him, step out, and come forward in faith in Him, it will be Jesus who will actually intercede for us, no matter how difficult the task may seem (Philippians 4:13). Jesus did this for Abraham and for us by becoming the sacrifice for the sin of mankind.

We can also see in Isaac a type of Christ in that he was fully submissive to his father Abraham. Like Jesus, Isaac laid his life down willingly on that altar. How do we know this? How do we know that Isaac was willing to be sacrificed by his father? It has been estimated that Isaac could have been thirty three years old at this time, this was Jesus' age at the time of His crucifixion. That would make Abraham one hundred and thirty three (Abraham was one hundred years old when Isaac was born, Genesis 21:5). There is no way a one hundred thirty three year old man could subdue a thirty three year old man and force him onto an altar to become a sacrifice. Therefore, Isaac must have submitted to his father's desire. Also it is important to remember here that when Abraham left his servants behind, before he and Isaac went up to the mountain, Abraham told them, *"Stay here with the donkey; the lad and I will go yonder and worship, and **we will come back to you**."* Genesis 22:5. (Emphasis added) Abraham was sure this whole situation would work out. Didn't Abraham already have God's promise that *"for in Isaac your seed shall be called"* (Genesis 21:12b)?

"But who do you say that I am?"

*"Then Abraham lifted his eyes and looked, and there behind him was a **ram caught in a thicket** by its horns. So Abraham went and took the ram, and offered it up for a burnt offering instead of his son"* (Genesis 22:13-emphasis added).

Now after Abraham was prevented from sacrificing his son Isaac by Jesus, the Angel of the LORD, Abraham then looks behind him and he sees a ram (an adult) *"caught in a thicket"* (verse 13). One can see the significance of Jesus' crown of thorns in this. Once again Jesus is reminding us of God's promise and His fulfillment to redeem us and Abraham's prophetic utterance to this in verse 8.

While writing this section of the book I had the clear sense that the altar that Abraham used for this sacrifice was on Calvary, not on what is know today as "Temple Mount," where the First and Second Temples were built and traditionally declared as the site of Abraham's altar. Later I learned from a friend who had been on a tour to Calvary that the guide for their group pointed out to them that Calvary was once part of Mount Moriah (also known today as Temple Mount).

Mount Moriah was the place where God had led Abraham to build the altar for sacrificing Isaac, and where the ram became the substitute sacrifice for Isaac. Could it very well be that the earthquake generated at the time of Jesus' death on the cross when the veil in the Temple split (Matthew 27:51) was the very one that caused Calvary to split away from what we know today as Temple Mount (Mt. Moriah)?

In conclusion, then, what better way to end this wonderful story of faith, submission and obedience of Abraham and Isaac than with the promise of Jesus' return one day. It is of no coincidence, I believe, that after this passage in Genesis 22 we do not hear anymore about Isaac until he meets his bride Rebecca (Genesis 24:64-66). And how does this refer to Jesus' return? We see that promise in Revelation 19:7-9 where the Bible tells us, *"Let us be glad and rejoice and give Him glory, for the marriage of the Lamb has come, and His wife has made herself ready. And to her it was granted to be arrayed in fine linen, clean and bright, for the fine linen is the righteous acts of the saints. Then he said to me, "Write: 'Blessed are those who are called to the marriage supper of the Lamb!'" And he said to me, "These are the true sayings of God."'*

Just as Rebecca made herself ready for Isaac, you and I are to spend our remaining days, here on Earth, making ourselves ready for our Creator and Husband, Jesus, the Lamb and King. And, how do we do that? In the same way that we have been shown in the story of Abraham and Isaac, through

- faith (Luke 17:6; Romans 10:17; Hebrews 11:1),
- submission (to the power of the Holy Spirit-Philippians 2:12-13)
- obedience (John 14:15-16).

Maybe this story of Abraham and Isaac was one of the areas in Scripture that Jesus had explained about Himself to His disciples during their walk on the road to Emmaus that glorious Resurrection Day.
Halleluyah!!!

CHAPTER THREE

LORD OF HOSTS (OUR REDEEMER)

Isaiah 44:6
"Thus says the LORD, the King of Israel,
And his Redeemer, the LORD of hosts:
'I am the First and I am the Last;
Besides Me there is no God.

In Revelation 1:17 John tells us how Jesus identified Himself. *"And when I saw Him, I fell at His feet as dead. But He laid His right hand on me, saying to me, 'Do not be afraid; I am the First and the Last'"* (Emphasis added).

Redeemer

We can see clearly from Isaiah's verse above that not only is the LORD of hosts identified as the **"First and the Last"** but as the "Redeemer" (Jesus) whom John saw in Revelation 1:17.

And, certainly one of the ways God displayed His redemptive power is in the story of Israel's deliverance from

"But who do you say that I am?"

Egypt, as recorded in the Old Testament, which pointed to the ultimate Redemption through Jesus Christ.

Let us review this wonderful story of deliverance and look for Jesus' manifestations throughout this classic example of salvation and deliverance by the "LORD of hosts."

Here we have God's chosen people in bondage to Pharaoh in Egypt until God sends them Moses, a son of Hebrew slaves brought up by Pharaoh's daughter and educated under the Egyptian system. We can associate their bondage in Egypt with our own lives because we were under the bondage to sin prior to our deliverance by faith in Jesus.

In my personal bondage to the world of sin, prior to receiving Jesus into my life and the Power of the Holy Spirit to direct my life, I was very successful, from a worldly standpoint, but dead inside spiritually. Then when all that success was taken away, followed by a severe battle with depression and a subsequent suicide attempt, I cried out to God for forgiveness and He miraculously delivered me from death and my bondage and set me free (John 8:32).

Then God brought people into my life to guide me (much like Moses, whom God had redeemed from the wilderness to guide Israel) and He delivered me from a life of bondage to sin.

Similarly, you can see when Moses brought the Israelites out of Egypt and then took them into the desert wilderness to receive the Law at the mountain of God; one would think that would be all that is needed. God would be their Husband (Isaiah 54:5) and everyone would live happily ever after. This was not so. Even though the "LORD of hosts" delivered them out of Egypt, they still needed to turn away and leave the world of Egypt behind them, including Egypt's system of gods, "principalities and powers," and all the worldly influences that still remained in the Hebrews at that time.

In my case, after I was delivered from the bondage of sin in my life, I still had to face that "wilderness" known as life

"But who do you say that I am?"

along with the same seemingly insurmountable problems I had before being saved by God through Jesus Christ. Then I had to turn away from all those things that were wrong in my life that separated me from becoming "holy" (1 Peter 15-16) and from the plan God had for my life (Jeremiah 29:11).

It is a process for us, just as it was for Israel in the desert for those 40 years. However, Jesus has given us the Holy Spirit (John 14:16) to be our "Helper." Like the Israelites, we cannot become holy or worthy by our own strength. We need God's help.

This is a "process," that is to say, the sanctification process that God bestows on us when we ask for and receive His Holy Spirit. The Holy Spirit then works in us *"to will and to do for His good pleasure"* (Philippians 2:13).

As an example of this "process," the following is an excerpt from my book "Ransomed: Let the redeemed of the LORD say so…" (pages 29-30)

"Other areas of my life that were not right with God took longer to change, only because I would not let go of them right away. Thank God for His patience with me. For example, I used to love to gamble, and at the time, I didn't believe it affected anyone but me. But as the Holy Spirit started to convict me that this behavior grieved Him, the fleshly desire in me started to fight back. I remember rationalizing—never try to rationalize with God, because you will lose every time—Well, I won't gamble in the United States anymore, because someone I know might see me. But if I gamble where no one knows me, I am just affecting myself. Right? Wrong! As I have learned, someone is always watching us, and our behavior is a testimony of whether we are partnering with God in our lives or not.

33

"But who do you say that I am?"

In a rare time that Ginny and I were able to get away by ourselves after my attempted suicide, we went to the Bahamas for a short vacation. Of course, I headed for the casino and some blackjack, which I thought I loved to play. However, this time I was not enjoying it even though I was winning. I could not put my finger on the reason, but somehow I felt it was not right. After we had returned to the states, I was driving our car and listening to a Christian radio station, where I heard Pastor Tony Evans preaching on why gambling is a sin. Tony used the playing of lotto, which I had also enjoyed, as an example of why gambling is a sin and of how gambling negatively effects others.

In his example, Tony explained that many people who play lotto are poor, and a winner is taking money from them. When we condone this practice, we were drawing others into to it, especially those with the most to lose. That sermon convicted me on the spot, and soon afterward my gambling days ended.

Someone reading this might ask, "You mean when we accept Jesus into our lives we have to give up all the fun things of life?" First, what I have learned is that this life is not about me, it is about my Savior, who died for me that I may live with Him in glory for all eternity. Second, this life is temporary. We are just sojourners here being refined like silver and gold, getting the "dross" removed—that stuff in our lives that gets between God and us. Like my career, for example, that so consumed me that I sacrificed the good things of this life, God, family and friends for it. If we never come to this realization, we are just living our lives for "things." Jesus said, *"For what profit is it to a man if he gains the whole world,*

"But who do you say that I am?"

and loses his own soul? Or what will a man give in exchange for his soul?" (Matthew 16:26).

This transformation included separating me from a sinful behavior (a process which will continue, thankfully, since I am not there yet). As Paul said in Philippians 1:6, *"Being confident of this very thing, that He who has begun a good work in you will complete it until the day of Jesus Christ."*

During that long 40 years of "wandering" in the desert, the LORD God gave Israel a standard to look to and to have faith in that God was in control, even over death. One can see this reference to Jesus and His being our "standard" today in Numbers 21:4-9. Here we see Israel's unbelief manifesting itself by their complaining "against God and Moses." They longed to have the things of Egypt again. They were now tired of the manna, that heavenly food, which had sustained them so far. One could compare this to the times we find it difficult to be in God's word which is our "heavenly food" today.

It was only a few chapters previous to this complaining (Chapters 13 & 14) where we see the children of Israel at the gate of the Promised Land but not entering because of unbelief that God would conquer the Land for them. They believed the "evil" reports of the ten spies, instead of believing Caleb and Joshua who had faith that God would prevail for them (Numbers 14:7-9). Now the children of Israel would have to wander in the wilderness for 40 years until this unbelieving generation was gone (Numbers 14:32-34).

Israel now frustrated because of the consequence of their unbelief and sentenced to forty years in the desert, sees no advantage to continue to be under God's rule (through Moses) anymore and now wonder why Moses took them out of Egypt in the first place (Numbers 21:5).

35

"But who do you say that I am?"

God hearing their complaint sends the "fiery serpents" into Israel's camp and when bitten by them, many Israelites die (v6). Here we have a prime example of what occurs when we turn away from God. Sin (as represented here by the fiery serpents) overtakes us and we may die. However, when we have *"godly sorrow,"* it produces repentance *"leading to salvation, not to be regretted; but the sorrow of the world produces death"* (2 Corinthians 7:10).

> *"Therefore the people came to Moses, and said, 'We have sinned* (godly sorrow), *for we have spoken against the LORD and against you; pray to the LORD that He take away the serpents from us.' So Moses prayed for the people.*
> *Then the LORD said to Moses, 'Make a fiery serpent, and set it on a pole; and it shall be that everyone who is bitten, when he looks at it, shall live.' So Moses made a bronze serpent, and put it on a pole; and so it was, if a serpent had bitten anyone, when he looked at the bronze serpent, he lived'"* (Numbers 21:7-9).

Here we can see, by faith (looking at the serpent on the pole), any Israelite bitten shall be saved from death through faith by fixing their gaze on the bronze serpent. This is that same faith pointing to our Redeemer who was lifted up onto the cross, taking our place, so that all who believe in Him shall be saved (John 3:16). Jesus Himself referred to this very example when He said, *"And as Moses lifted up the serpent in the wilderness, even so must the Son of Man be lifted up, that whoever believes in Him should not perish but have eternal life"* (John 3:14-15).

Now when Israel finally reached the Promised Land it was not Moses who led them into it. It was Joshua, whose name in Hebrew was "Yeshua," meaning "Savior," reminding us

"But who do you say that I am?"

once again of our Savior and Redeemer, the LORD of hosts, Jesus, who will lead us into our "Promised Land" when our journey here in the wilderness on earth is completed. Halleluyah!!!

LORD of hosts

In the New King James version of the Bible there are some 245 occurrences for the references to Jesus as the "LORD of hosts" and 18 occurrences for "Redeemer" introduced to us in Isaiah 44:6 at the beginning of this chapter. These references span 14 chapters in the Old Testament and so far we have only looked at one connection to the Redeemer, Jesus. Imagine how many books it would take to cover Jesus in all the remaining verses. In any case we will look at one more verse and subsequent reference to Jesus focusing this time on the Lord Jesus as the "LORD of hosts."

In the story of Elijah's victory on Mt. Carmel we can see the prominent role Jesus (LORD of hosts) played in proving to Israel and to the Gentiles (represented by the Baal worshipers) that He is the true God (1 Kings 18:40). But first let us take a close look at the verse from Isaiah which prefaced this chapter.

"Thus says the LORD, the King of Israel, And his Redeemer, the LORD of hosts:
'I am the First and I am the Last; Besides Me there is no God.'" (Isaiah 44:6)

It is God talking to us. When one sees LORD in all capital letters it is the sovereign Name of God in the Bible: "YAH." Now let us look more closely at what God says in this verse: "Thus says the LORD (YAH), the King of Israel, **And his Redeemer**, the LORD of hosts (emphasis added). Clearly here we are talking of the first two manifestations of the Godhead,

37

"But who do you say that I am?"

the Father and His Son. *"I and My Father are one"* (John 10:30). The "LORD of hosts" is also our "Redeemer" and "LORD." Our YAH, our Messiah, and our Salvation! This verse is so packed with Jesus, one must rejoice with its revelation. *"Sing to God, sing praises to His name; Extol Him who rides on the clouds, By His name YAH, And rejoice before Him"* (Psalm 68:4). As the disciples on the road to Emmaus said, after the revelation of Jesus to them, *"Did not our heart burn within us while He talked with us on the road, and while He opened the Scriptures to us?"* (Luke 24:32)

Now let us look at one more verse about the LORD of hosts before we continue our revelation of Jesus in the story of Elijah on Mt. Carmel.

*"So let it be established, that Your name may be magnified forever, saying, 'The LORD of hosts, the **God of Israel, is Israel's God.**' And let the house of **Your servant David** be established before You"* (1 Chronicles 17:24-emphasis added).

Here we see Jesus (LORD of hosts) is also the "God of Israel" and "Israel's God." Clearly, "your servant David" is in reference to Jesus' kingdom being established through King David's Seed who is, of course, Jesus Christ (Luke 3:23-38). Since Jesus is Israel's God, it only makes sense that when God became Man to save us from our sins that He would be born of His chosen people, Israel.

Now in the story of Elijah, God sends Elijah to Ahab the king of Israel who has led Israel into idolatry to forsake the true God of Israel. As Elijah said, *"As the **LORD of hosts** lives, before whom I stand, I will surely present myself to him today"* (1 Kings 18:15-emphasis added). It was Elijah's job to show and demonstrate to Ahab and all Israel who the true God is and save them from the evil king who has led them astray.

38

"But who do you say that I am?"

"Then it happened, when Ahab saw Elijah, that Ahab said to him, 'Is that you, O troubler of Israel?'
And he answered, 'I have not troubled Israel, but you and your father's house have, in that you have forsaken the commandments of the LORD and have followed the Baals. Now therefore, send and gather all Israel to me on Mount Carmel, the four hundred and fifty prophets of Baal, and the four hundred prophets of Asherah, who eat at Jezebel's table'" (1 Kings 18:17-19).

We can see this event pointing to our ultimate redemption through Christ when Jesus said, *"For God so loved the world that He gave His only begotten Son, that whoever believes in Him should not perish but have everlasting life"* (John 3:16). It is certainly no coincidence that it is Jesus Himself (LORD of hosts) that is sending Elijah on this prophetic mission to save all Israel. Elijah is also putting his life on the line. However, it is his faith in the "LORD of hosts" that saves Elijah and Israel, as we shall see, just as our faith in Jesus saves us.

After all of Israel and the false prophets reach the summit of Mount Carmel, Elijah says, *"How long will you falter between two opinions? If the LORD is God, follow Him; but if Baal, follow him."* But the people answered him not a word" (1 Kings 18:21).

In our world today, we have a similar attitude. Many believe there are many paths to God or "Spirituality." But Jesus said, *"I am the way, the truth, and the life. No one comes to the Father except through Me"* (John 14:6). Jesus even sacrificed Himself for us on Mt. Calvary so that we would know that He is the Ultimate Sacrifice that gives us the "Way" and reconciles us to our Father in Heaven.

Prophetically pointing to Jesus, we now have Elijah getting ready to offer a sacrifice that will turn the hearts of

"But who do you say that I am?"

his people back to God on this day. As Elijah prepares this sacrifice it is important to realize that Elijah is more than a prophet, he must have been a priest. Only the priests of his day could offer sacrifices. However, Elijah, from what we know, was not of the tribe of Levi or in the lineage of Aaron. In fact, there is no lineage to be found in the Bible for Elijah. The only other person in the Old Testament with no lineage was Melchizedek, king of Salem (Genesis 14:18). Therefore, one can assume that Elijah was from this priestly order of Melchizedek where Jesus is the High Priest (Hebrews 5:10).

As we continue this account of Elijah, he is now with the king of Israel, the prophets of Baal and all of the people of Israel have their eyes fixed on this bold prophet of God. *"Then Elijah said to the people, 'I alone am left a prophet of the LORD; but Baal's prophets are four hundred and fifty men. Therefore let them give us two bulls; and let them choose one bull for themselves, cut it in pieces, and lay it on the wood, but put no fire under it; and I will prepare the other bull, and lay it on the wood, but put no fire under it. Then you call on the name of your gods, and I will call on the name of the LORD; and the God who answers by fire, He is God.' So all the people answered and said, 'It is well spoken'"* (1 Kings 18:22-24).

The prophets of Baal prepared their sacrifice and then called on their gods, most of the day as it turned out, but no gods answered them. About noon time Elijah mocked them and said, *"Cry aloud, for he is a god; either he is meditating, or he is busy, or he is on a journey, or perhaps he is sleeping and must be awakened."*

So they cried aloud, and cut themselves, as was their custom, with knives and lances, until the blood gushed out on them'" (1 Kings 18:27-28). This continued until the time of the evening sacrifice when Elijah finally called the people close to him.

"But who do you say that I am?"

The first thing Elijah did, *"...he repaired the altar of the LORD that was broken down"* (1 Kings 18:30). When Jesus was preaching to His disciples about His second coming He said, *"Indeed, Elijah is coming first and will restore all things"* (Matthew 17:11). Amos also prophesied about this "restoration" when he said, *"On that day I will raise up The tabernacle of David, which has fallen down, And repair its damages; I will raise up its ruins, And rebuild it as in the days of old; That they may possess the remnant of Edom, And all the Gentiles who are called by My name," Says the LORD who does this thing"* (Amos 9:11-12).

Elijah is now about to restore his people Israel to their God but this event also points ahead to the day prophesied by Isaiah in 45:23 when God said, *"I have sworn by Myself; The word has gone out of My mouth in righteousness, And shall not return, That to Me every knee shall bow, Every tongue shall take an oath."* This is also restated in Philippians 2:10-11, *"that at the name of Jesus every knee should bow, of those in heaven, and of those on earth, and of those under the earth, and that every tongue should confess that Jesus Christ is Lord, to the glory of God the Father."* Halleluyah!!!

Now at this point, *"Elijah took twelve stones, according to the number of the tribes of the sons of Jacob, to whom the word of the LORD had come, saying, "Israel shall be your name." Then with the stones he built an altar in the name of the LORD; and he made a trench around the altar large enough to hold two seahs of seed. And he put the wood in order, cut the bull in pieces, and laid it on the wood, and said, "Fill four water pots with water, and pour it on the burnt sacrifice and on the wood." Then he said, "Do it a second time," and they did it a second time; and he said, "Do it a third time," and they did it a third time. So the water ran all around the altar; and he also filled the trench with water"* (1 Kings 18:31-35).

As an aside, on the highest point of Mount Carmel today there is a church called Carmel Assembly. It is a wonderful church open to all believers. If you get a chance to visit Israel it is worth the trip to Haifa to worship with the body of Christ at the Carmel Assembly Church. What is so special about it is that one can go there and see Arab and Jewish believers in Jesus worshipping together. The sanctuary is surrounded by twelve stones representing the twelve tribes of Israel. And, above the sanctuary is a glass ceiling symbolizing the open sky over Elijah's altar. There are also ten beams in the ceiling representing the Ten Commandments. And the doorways represent the priest's breastplates with openings in the doors representing the precious stones of those breastplates. It is a beautiful church, but what makes it wonderful are all the saints that come together and worship there and the welcoming they give to strangers visiting this lovely church.

Now with the altar of the LORD restored, the sacrificed prepared, Elijah prayed at the time of the evening sacrifice. *"LORD God of Abraham, Isaac, and Israel, let it be known this day that You are God in Israel and I am Your servant, and that I have done all these things at Your word. Hear me, O LORD, hear me, that this people may know that You are the LORD God, and that You have turned their hearts back to You again"* (1 Kings 18:36-37).

We also see this prayer of repentance repeated at the time of the evening sacrifice after Ezra restored the Temple in Jerusalem (Ezra 9:5-15). And again we see the contrite heart of Daniel in his prayer for his people (Daniel 9:4-19) before their return from Babylon. Repentance is key to salvation as we see from Jesus' teachings; *"Now after John was put in prison, Jesus came to Galilee, preaching the gospel of the kingdom of God, and saying, "The time is fulfilled, and the kingdom of God is at hand. Repent, and believe in the gospel"* (Mark 1:14-15). Repentance always precedes Salvation as

"But who do you say that I am?"

we see in 2 Corinthians 7:10; *"For **godly sorrow** produces **repentance** leading to **salvation**, not to be regretted; but the sorrow of the world produces death"* (Emphasis added).

It is certainly of no coincidence that in the same Chapter 9 of Daniel's prayer, referenced above, is the prophecy of the coming of Jesus, the Messiah. *"Know therefore and understand, That from the going forth of the command To restore and build Jerusalem Until Messiah the Prince, There shall be seven weeks and sixty-two weeks; The street shall be built again, and the wall, Even in troublesome times"* (Daniel 9:25).

Now as we return to Elijah on Mount Carmel, after he had prayed to God, we see how God answered him in a mighty way by turning the hearts of the Israelites back to their God. *"Then the fire of the LORD fell and consumed the burnt sacrifice, and the wood and the stones and the dust, and it licked up the water that was in the trench. Now when all the people saw it, they fell on their faces; and they said, 'The LORD, He is God! The LORD, He is God!'"* (1 Kings 18:38-39).

These miracles in Moses' and Elijah's day have two significant meanings for us:

1. Through Moses we see the deliverance of Israel from the bondage of Egypt (through the Red Sea) and eventual possession of the Promised Land. These events point ahead to when Jesus would deliver us from the bondage of sin (through His blood) and into Paradise with Him for all eternity.

2. Through Elijah, as a type Melchizedek priest (Christophany), we see the preparing of the sacrifice on the restored altar of God that returned God's believing children back to their Father and restoring the kingdom to Him. These events pointing to our High

43

Priest (Jesus), according to the order of Melchizedek, sacrificing Himself in order to reconcile all believers to God and preparing the way for the restoration of the tabernacle and throne of David where Jesus is King of kings and Lord of lords. Halleluyah!!!

*"Of the increase of His government and peace, There will be no end, Upon the throne of David and over His kingdom, To order it and establish it with judgment and justice From that time forward, even forever. The zeal of the **Lord of hosts** will perform this."* (Isaiah 9:7-emphasis added).

The significance of Moses and Elijah in their roles for the unfolding of God's plan for man's redemption is why, I believe, Jesus included these two obedient men of God when He was transfigured before Peter, James and John on Mount Tabor.

"Now after six days Jesus took Peter, James, and John, and led them up on a high mountain apart by themselves; and He was transfigured before them. His clothes became shining, exceedingly white, like snow, such as no launderer on earth can whiten them. And Elijah appeared to them with Moses, and they were talking with Jesus" (Mark 9:2-4). In Luke's account of this same appearance of Jesus in His glory, Luke tells us what they were talking about. *"And behold, two men talked with Him, who were Moses and Elijah, who appeared in glory and spoke of His decease which He was about to accomplish at Jerusalem"* (Luke 9:30-31).

It seems very likely that of the many Scriptures that Jesus could have expounded on about Himself to His disciples,

"But who do you say that I am?"

these two major events would have been included. They convey His message of salvation through not only His word but also through the lives of His faithful servants, Moses and Elijah. This is the way God has consistently fulfilled His plans, through His chosen people. Halleluyah!!!

CHAPTER FOUR

SON OF MAN

Daniel 7:13-14
"I was watching in the night visions,
And behold, one like the Son of Man,
Coming with the clouds of heaven!
He came to the Ancient of Days,
And they brought Him near before Him.

Then to Him was given dominion and
glory and a kingdom, That all peoples,
nations, and languages should serve Him.
His dominion is an everlasting dominion,
Which shall not pass away, And His kingdom
the one Which shall not be destroyed.

Jesus referred to Himself as the "Son of Man" some 87 times in the New Testament. We can see from the above verses how Daniel prophesied very clearly about Jesus' appearance as "one like the Son of Man." We know Daniel is referring to Jesus because this is how Jesus said He would return to claim His kingdom. *"Jesus said to him, "It is as you said. Nevertheless, I say to you, hereafter you will see the Son of Man sitting at the right hand of the Power, and coming on the clouds of heaven"* (Matthew 26:64).

Why this title? After all, Jesus is the Lord of lords and King of kings (Revelation 17:14). Before we answer this question, however, let us look at how the son of man is referred to in the Old Testament. Specifically we can get an idea from Psalm 8:4 where the Bible says, *"What is man that You are mindful of him, And the son of man that You visit him?"* To me, this verse conveys how insignificant I am, a piece of dust at most, in comparison to God. Yet Jesus became the "Son of man" to serve, not to be served, so that we may be restored to our Father through Him.

In the previous book I have mentioned earlier, "Ransomed: Let the redeemed of the LORD say so..." (pages 49-53), I shared an experience I had that really taught me about the "fear of God" and ultimately the humility I needed to learn if I intended to serve our Lord. This opportunity to share my experiences with you is a blessing, although such a minor effort toward describing the awesome characteristics of the "Son of man."

"Going Deeper

Though the Lord was using me to reach others through the testimony He had given me, I still had (and still have) a lot to learn about Him. However, He soon revealed to me that even more important than knowing about Him was coming to know Him in a deeper way. This deeper revelation came to me while I was traveling to see my daughter Sue and her family in Oregon. It would instill in me the "fear of God," the reverence and honor that is due our Sovereign and Almighty God. It came in a way that I will never forget and that will always remind me, I pray, never to take my God for granted.

48

"But who do you say that I am?"

On the way to Oregon, I picked up my sister, Laurie, in Denver, and we traveled together to Jackson Hole, Wyoming, to do some camping. Laurie instilled the love of hiking in me there, and we proceeded to hike halfway around Lake Genny and up into the mountains a little way(s). It was a time of reconnecting with Laurie after many years of being away in my own world fulfilling selfish desires. It was a wonderful time together and a blessing!

After a few days of enjoying this most beautiful part of the world, Laurie returned to her home in Colorado while I continued on to see Sue and her family. But first I wanted to finish the hike around the lake that Laurie and I had started.

If you have ever been to Jackson, Wyoming, you will understand that words are not enough to describe the beauty and strength of the mountains there. I believe the power and majesty of God are visible in those mountains. It is beyond me that anyone can look at this wonderful world that God created for us and not believe in Him. What a tragedy not to enjoy Him and His creation for us.

The day started out bright and sunny. The first part of my hike was at the base of the mountains; then as I came to the side of the lake that Laurie and I had not completed, I found myself looking right into those mountains. It was a magnificent sight. I remember looking at the two mountains in front of me with a valley between them and being almost frozen in my tracks by the beauty of this sight.

The sky was completely overcast now. It was a solid overcast. There were no individual clouds, just a gray sky overhead. Then I saw it. It was a puff of a cloud that appeared between the two majestic mountains, ascended to the mountain peak to my left, and

49

"But who do you say that I am?"

encircled its peak. I thought, this must be something like what the children of Israel witnessed when they came to the Mountain of God in the desert before receiving the Ten Commandments from God.

Then this puff of a cloud descended the mountain, came to the center of the lake, and hovered directly in front of me. It was then that I realized that something special was taking place. When this cloud was encircling the mountain peak, I wondered if it could be an angel. Now I was sure it was because he seemed to be looking directly at me as he hovered over the lake. I don't know what possessed me, but I took a picture of him, but then he retreated to the far side of the lake. This sudden departure by the angel made me feel irreverent in taking a picture at the special moment of our meeting.

Next, the small cloud linked up with and started to follow a much larger cloud. Immediately I knew I was in the presence of God and dropped to my knees. Then the battle started in my mind. "You're kneeling on this path. What if someone comes along and finds you like this." I listened to that voice, so I stood up. Then the power of God overwhelmed me, and I remember thinking, I am in the presence of God, and I am worried about what someone else thinks! I dropped to my knees and stayed there. During that time, I had the sense of what an insignificant speck of dust I was in the presence of God Almighty. I could now understand how the children of Israel felt when they said to Moses, *"You speak with us, and we will hear; but let not God speak with us, lest we die"* (Exodus 20:19). I hate to admit this, but I wanted to leave this place as soon as I could. I felt so unworthy and afraid to be in His Holy Presence.

"But who do you say that I am?"

But it was as if I was nailed to that spot. I couldn't get up and run away as I wanted to. Then the angel escorted the Lord from my sight but returned in that puff of a cloud that seemed to cover him. He hovered over the lake one last time until, all of a sudden, he seemed to send something like two silver arrows in my direction. Then he disappeared.

As I got off my knees, two hikers came down the path from the opposite direction I had been traveling and went by me. It was (as) if time had restarted after standing still while I was in the presence of our King. All I could do was just about run from that spot while looking over my shoulder as I went down the path.

Whatever I had envisioned God to be before, I now knew He was beyond what I could ever imagine and that He required of me all the reverence, respect, and honor that is due Him. It was time to come to know Him, not just to know about Him. In looking back now on this epiphany in my life, it was time to fix my eyes on Jesus, the personification of God, if I was ever going to know God in a personal and loving way.

Fortunately, when we accept Jesus into our lives, He gives us His Holy Spirit to work in us those changes needed for us to come into that deeper relationship with God. He provides the righteousness that covers us, which is needed so when we stand in our Father's presence, He sees Jesus, not our *"filthy rags.'"*

One thing that experience shows to me is how far I am from the humility of Jesus. He displayed to us that ultimate humility by casting off His robes of glory and taking a position among men as the "Son of Man" but even more than that, becoming a servant to man. Jesus said, *"For even the*

"But who do you say that I am?"

Son of Man did not come to be served, but to serve, and to give His life a ransom for many" (Mark 10:45).

While Jesus was on this Earth He did not set Himself up as greater than anyone else, even though He was God Almighty in the flesh. Jesus was the perfect example of humility and obedience to His Father's will, not His own will ("thy will be done"). Jesus lived with us (Acts 1:21), worked with us (Matthew 13:55), taught us (John 18:20), rejoiced with us (Luke 10:21), cried with us (John 11:35), loved us (Mark 10:21), was angry with us (Mark 11:15), and was tempted as we are (Matthew 4:1-11), but He did not sin (Hebrews 4:15). He died (John 19:30), but was raised so we could be reconciled to our Father and receive an eternal inheritance forever (1 Peter 1:3-4). Jesus' entire mission on earth was to bring glory to His Father by his obedience to Him (John 17:4) in bringing redemption to all men, as the "Son of Man." As the old hymn goes, "What a Friend we have in Jesus!" Halleluyah!

In fact, there is almost twice the emphasis in the Gospels about Jesus being the "Son of Man" than there is about Him being the "Son of God." A conclusion that can be drawn from this is that Jesus was presenting to us how God created us and wants us to reflect His image to others. God did not create us to be the "Son of God," as there is only "One God." However, Jesus gives us, through the redemption and reconciliation to God, the honor of becoming the adoptive *"sons of God"* (Luke 20:36).

Now let us look at some ways the Bible describes Jesus as this "Son of Man."

The "Son of Man:"

- *"...And your righteousness the son of man"* (Job 35:8)

52

"But who do you say that I am?"

- *"...And the son of man that You visit him"* (Psalm 8:4)
- *"...Upon the son of man whom You made strong for yourself"* (Psalm 80:17)
- *"Blessed is the man who does this, And the son of man who lays hold on it; Who keeps from defiling the Sabbath, And keeps his hand from doing any evil."* (Isaiah 56:2)
- *"...And behold, one like the Son of Man, coming with clouds of heaven!"* (Daniel 7:13)
- *"...has nowhere to lay His head."* (Matthew 8:20)
- *"...has power on earth to forgive sins"* (Matthew 9:6)
- *"Therefore the Son of Man is also Lord of the Sabbath."* (Mark 2:28)
- *"...The Son of Man is being betrayed into the hands of men, and they will kill Him. And after He is killed, He will rise the third day."* (Mark 9:31)
- *"For the Son of Man did not come to destroy men's lives but to save them..."* (Luke 9:56)
- *"For as Jonah became a sign to the Ninevites, so also the Son of Man will be to this generation."* (Luke 11:30)
- *"...hereafter you shall see heaven open, and the angels of God ascending and descending upon the Son of Man"* (John 1:51)
- *"And as Moses lifted up the serpent in the wilderness, even so must the Son of Man be lifted up,"* (John 3:14)
- *"...The hour has come that the Son of Man should be glorified."* (John 12:23)

We can conclude from this that God clearly defined His role here on earth as the humble servant "Son of Man." Directly relating to this, I believe, is the most important

"But who do you say that I am?"

prayer (and one of the shortest) in the whole Bible and it is found in Psalm 79:9.

*"Help us, O God of our salvation, for the glory of Your name; and deliver us, and **provide atonement for our sins**, For Your name's sake!"* (Emphasis added)

It seems that during the times of God's Holy Temple in Jerusalem someone understood the futility of animal sacrifices for the atonement of sins. And God heard and answered that prayer in the most powerful way by providing Himself, through the "Son of Man," as that atoning sacrifice, "a ransom for many."

"For even the Son of Man did not come to be served, but to serve, and to give His life a ransom for many" (Mark 10:45).

Thank You, Jesus! Halleluyah!!!

CHAPTER FIVE

MELCHIZEDEK

Genesis 14:18
Then Melchizedek king of Salem
brought out bread and wine;
he was the priest of God Most High.

Probably the most mysterious person in the Bible is King Melchizedek. Superficially, there certainly is not much known about him. However, when we allow God to reveal Himself through His word we will see Jesus in the Person of King Melchizedek. Could this be another area that Jesus expounded in Scriptures about Himself with His disciples on the road to Emmaus? Let us examine these Scriptures ourselves and learn a little more about our Dear Jesus.

We know, for example, Melchizedek was "the priest of the God Most High." We see this truth clearly stated in Genesis 14:18. Interestingly, the genealogy for King Melchizedek cannot be found anywhere in the Bible. We do know, however, that He was God manifested in the flesh because Abraham offered a tithe to King Melchizedek (Genesis 14:20). In all of the Bible, only God is offered tithes.

We can also see Jesus in King Melchizedek in these revealing words of Psalm 110:

"But who do you say that I am?"

"A Psalm of David

The LORD said to my Lord, "Sit at My right hand, Till I make Your enemies Your footstool."

2 The LORD shall send the rod of Your strength out of Zion. Rule in the midst of Your enemies!

3 Your people shall be volunteers In the day of Your power; In the beauties of holiness, from the womb of the morning, You have the dew of Your youth.

4 The LORD has sworn And will not relent, "You are a priest forever According to the order of Melchizedek."

5 The Lord is at Your right hand; He shall execute kings in the day of His wrath.

6 He shall judge among the nations, He shall fill the places with dead bodies, He shall execute the heads of many countries.

7 He shall drink of the brook by the wayside; Therefore He shall lift up the head."

"The LORD said to my Lord." Seeing "LORD" spelled entirely in capital letters in this passage is proof David is referring to YAHVH, the Tetrogram, or Holy name of God. David also writes about "my Lord," one of Jesus' known titles. How do we know "Lord" is one of Jesus' titles? We know because Jesus announced this in Matthew 22:41-45, when He asked the religious leaders of His day whose descendant they thought He was.

56

"But who do you say that I am?"

"While the Pharisees were gathered together, Jesus asked them, saying, *"What do you think about the Christ? Whose Son is He?" They said to Him, "The Son of David." He said to them, "How then does David in the Spirit call Him 'Lord,' saying: 'The LORD said to my Lord, "Sit at My right hand, Till I make Your enemies Your footstool"'? If David then calls Him 'Lord,' how is He his Son?"*

Now in verse four of David's Psalm, we see God (LORD) bestowing the special title of priest on Jesus by saying, *"You are a priest forever According to the order of Melchizedek."* We know this is a special priesthood because in the time of David the priests came from the line of Aaron and the tribe of Levi. Jesus was from the tribe of Judah. Why was God setting up a special priesthood outside the Levitical priesthood that He had established through Moses? The writer of the Book of Hebrews answers this question very well when he says:

> *"Seeing then that we have a great High Priest who has passed through the heavens, Jesus the Son of God, let us hold fast our confession. For we do not have a High Priest who cannot sympathize with our weaknesses, but was in all points tempted as we are, yet without sin. Let us therefore come boldly to the throne of grace that we may obtain mercy and find grace to help in time of need.*
>
> *Qualifications for High Priesthood: For every high priest taken from among men is appointed for men in things pertaining to God, that he may offer both gifts and sacrifices for sins. He can have compassion on those who are ignorant and going astray, since he himself is also subject to weakness. Because of this he is required as for the people, so also for himself, to offer sacrifices for sins. And no*

"But who do you say that I am?"

man takes this honor to himself, but he who is called by God, just as Aaron was.

A Priest Forever So also Christ did not glorify Himself to become High Priest, but it was He who said to Him: "You are My Son, Today I have begotten You." As He also says in another place: "You are a priest forever According to the order of Melchizedek;.. This hope we have as an anchor of the soul, both sure and steadfast, and which enters the Presence behind the veil, where the forerunner has entered for us, even Jesus, having become High Priest forever according to the order of Melchizedek" (Hebrews 4:14-5:6; 6:19-20).

We can see from these passages that the priesthood set up through Aaron was set up to intercede for man by offering animal sacrifices for the remission of sins, both for the priest and the people. It was a system God allowed in order to point His people of faith in Him to their promised Messiah. Jesus fulfilled that promise of our Messiah and ultimate sacrifice by being tempted as we are but He did not sin. Jesus became our perfect sacrifice, thus satisfying the requirement for the remission of our sins, once and for all time. He is now interceding for us in heaven as our High Priest in the order of Melchizedek.

Therefore, we can now be confident that we have a High Priest, Jesus Christ, interceding with the Father on our behalf so we can *"come boldly to the throne of grace that we may obtain mercy* (for our sins) *and find grace to help in time of need* (Hebrews 4:16-emphasis added); for it is God, who will work in us *'to will and to do for His good pleasure'* (Philippians 2:13).

Halleluyah!

CHAPTER SIX

SON OF GOD

๛

Proverbs 30:4
Who has ascended into heaven, or descended?
Who has gathered the wind in His fists?
Who has bound the waters in a garment?
Who has established all the ends of the earth?
What is His name, and
what is His Son's name,
If you know?

REVELATION

One of the most controversial aspects of Jesus' being is His Deity, in that He is God in the flesh. This must have been one of those Truths that "burned" within the hearts of His disciples that morning during their walk on the road to Emmaus. Jesus had met them that morning after His Resurrection to enlighten them and to open their eyes to see Him as their Lord and Savior, God Incarnate. Yet what is so clear from Scripture is that this Truth is revealed to us from our Father in Heaven and not from "flesh and blood."

When Jesus asked His disciples in Matthew 16:15, *"But who do you say that I am?"* Peter responded in the next verse, *"You are the Christ the Son of the living God."* Then Jesus made a remarkable statement to Peter in verse 17, *"Blessed are you, Simon Bar-Jonah, for flesh and blood has not revealed this to you, but My Father who is in heaven."*

This fact about Jesus being the Son of God, as well as being God Himself, is so important and is the "cornerstone" to our faith in God. Jesus was not going to leave it up to man to convince others of His Divinity, but only through our Father in heaven. That is why, I believe, Jesus forbade His disciples to reveal this truth about Himself to anyone (Matthew 16:20).

From my own experience, I do know how true it is that God does the revealing, not me. He may use us, work through us, but it is God, by the power of the Holy Spirit, that reveals and draws those who are to be saved to receive Jesus into their lives. The following testimony is again excerpted from the book, "Ransomed: Let the redeemed of the LORD say so..." (pages 53-54). My intention is to shed more light on this very critical point concerning revelation.

"Reaching Others

The Holy Spirit also works through us to reach others for Christ, sometimes in spite of ourselves. This became evident when I visited a long-time friend who did not know Jesus in a personal way. Bette Jo was into a lot of "new age" beliefs, so it should not have been a surprise to me that the Lord wanted to reach her. When we met in 1999, I had this tremendous urge to tell her about Jesus, but I felt inadequate in doing so. I was all hung up in what would be the right things to say. Would I remember the right Scripture to quote? and on and on. If only I had remembered what the Lord had told me earlier about how He would provide the words.

"But who do you say that I am?"

It was a frustrating time to say the least. At one point I blurted out, "Well, if you had the cure for cancer, wouldn't you want to tell others about it?" I could see I was getting nowhere, and if anything, I was just driving her farther away from her Savior. Finally, she had had enough and we parted, not even saying good-bye to each other. This mission was a total failure, and as I traveled down the highway, I told God I was sorry for being such a failure and wondered why He had even allowed me to talk to Bette Jo at all.

During Christmas time that year, which was a few months after my visit to see Bette Jo, I received this beautiful Christmas card from her and it had a verse from the Gospel of Luke about our Savior on it. It really surprised me, especially because she was not a believer but she sent this beautiful card anyway. I called her to thank her for being so thoughtful, and after we exchanged pleasantries, she proceeded to tell me about the incredible experience she had.

She said, "You know, after you left, I received 'The Jesus Film' in the mail." If you are not familiar with this movie on video cassette, it is about who Jesus is and why we need Him as our Savior. Its powerful message from the Book of Luke, which has been translated into many languages, has been used by our Lord to bring thousands to Christ around the world. I should have realized what was coming next from Bette Jo, but I am ashamed to say I was expecting the worst. She continued, "Well, I looked at that tape, and at the end they give the sinner's prayer. And you know what?" (I was hanging on her every word now.) "I said it."

All I could say at this point was, Praise God! No other words came into my mind but "Praise God!" I

"But who do you say that I am?"

just kept saying, "Praise God!" It was truly the work of the Holy Spirit, not me. Then she said, "You know, if you had not talked to me that day, I would never have looked at that tape." It was from this experience that I learned that the Holy Spirit will work through us in spite of ourselves. He just wants a willing spirit to work with. Later I learned that "The Jesus Film" had arrived—the very day we parted!

Bette Jo continues to grow in the Lord, and recently she told me she met the pastor who was responsible for sending out "The Jesus Film" at that perfect time for her to receive it. What a blessing that must have been. And I thank that pastor for his obedience to our Lord in taking that brave step to send out the Lord's tape to many in the area, in pure faith that it would reach others for Him. Praise God!!!"

From this wonderful outcome to the testimony of Bette Jo's revelation of Jesus, I learned a very valuable lesson; *"For it is God who works in you, both to will and to do for His good pleasure"* (Philippians 2:13). And as Jesus clearly said, *"I am the vine, you are the branches. He who abides in Me, and I in him, bears much fruit; for without Me you can do nothing"* (John 15:5). I am a tool God can use if He so desires, but I am not the savior and cannot save anyone let alone myself.

This knowledge has really transformed and made my walk with the Lord easier. It removed the pressure that comes with our responsibility to witness to others about Jesus. I had always felt I needed to be sure to have the right Scriptures and facts memorized before talking about the Lord with anyone, whether with non-believers or even believers. I now know that the Lord will not bring a person to be saved onto my path without His equipping me for that ordained moment. He will not allow us to fail. *"I will triumph in the works of*

62

"But who do you say that I am?"

Your hands" (Psalm 92:4b). Praise God in His infinite love for us!

SON OF GOD

We can see Jesus referred to as the "Son of God" in the Old Testament in the beautiful story in the Book of Daniel about Shadrach, Meshach and Abed-Nego (Daniel 3). These three young Jewish men would not compromise their obedience and belief in God, even with the threat of death in a fiery furnace. It is a story which carries an important message of faith and trust in the Son of God, even for us today.

"Nebuchadnezzar the king made an image of gold, whose height was sixty cubits and its width six cubits. He set it up in the plain of Dura, in the province of Babylon. And King Nebuchadnezzar sent word to gather together the satraps, the administrators, the governors, the counselors, the treasurers, the judges, the magistrates, and all the officials of the provinces, to come to the dedication of the image which King Nebuchadnezzar had set up... that at the time you hear the sound of the horn, flute, harp, lyre, and psaltery, in symphony with all kinds of music, you shall fall down and worship the gold image that King Nebuchadnezzar has set up; (Daniel 3:1-2,5).

"Therefore at that time certain Chaldeans came forward and accused the Jews" (Daniel 3:8). King Nebuchadnezzar became furious when this was reported to him and he ordered the three Jewish men to be brought to him. After the king gave Shadrach, Meshach and Abed-Nego one more chance to bow down and worship his idol, which they refused to do, the king then ordered them to be thrown into a fiery oven. In fact, the oven was so hot that the men who had thrown

63

"But who do you say that I am?"

the three of God's faithful perished in flame of the fire even though they were outside of the oven.

Before being thrown into the furnace these three devout men of God made a statement of faith that we should all meditate on in order to incorporate it into our hearts.

"Shadrach, Meshach, and Abed-nego answered and said to the king, 'O Nebuchadnezzar, we have no need to answer you in this matter. If that is the case, our God whom we serve is able to deliver us from the burning fiery furnace, and He will deliver us from your hand, O king. But if not, let it be known to you, O king, that we do not serve your gods, nor will we worship the gold image which you have set up'" (Daniel 3:16-18).

What is exceptional about their statement is that even if God did not deliver them from the "fiery furnace" they would not worship the king's idol. What trust and faith in God they had. Would we respond in the way they did? We should because Jesus has said, *"These things I have spoken to you, that in Me you may have peace. In the world you will have tribulation; but be of good cheer, I have overcome the world"* (John 16:33). And in Psalm 91:10-11 God promises us, *"No evil shall befall you, Nor shall any plague come near your dwelling; For He shall give His angels charge over you, To keep you in all your ways."*

These three godly men's position against worshipping the king's idol did not keep them from the fiery furnace. In fact, they were thrown into the fire bound with their clothes on. This should have only added to their incineration, but the LORD God, who is true to His word miraculously saved them from even being singed by the fire.

64

"But who do you say that I am?"

*"And these three men, Shadrach, Meshach, and Abed-nego, fell down bound into the midst of the burning fiery furnace. Then King Nebuchadnezzar was astonished; and he rose in haste and spoke, saying to his counselors, 'Did we not cast three men bound into the midst of the fire?' They answered and said to the king, 'True, O king.' 'Look!' he answered, 'I see four men loose, walking in the midst of the fire; and they are not hurt, and the form of the fourth is like the **Son of God**'"* (Daniel 3:23-25-emphasis added).

Pausing here for a moment, I want to point out that this passage from Daniel points out a very important truth about our relationship with the "Son of God." We may not be kept from our trials and tribulations (fiery furnace) but we can always depend on Jesus going through them with us and bringing us through them. I have discovered this in my own experiences and I would like to share with you what I have discovered about suffering in general.

Suffering

Another powerful lesson the Lord taught me was about suffering, and this time He used my grandson Xavier, my daughter Julie's and her husband Keith's oldest son. But first I would like to comment on what I believe to be at least three reasons for suffering in this life: (1) our sin, (2) the benefit of others, (3) our growth.

First, suffering comes as a result of our sin, our wrong choices (John 5:14). It is true Jesus paid the penalty for our sins; however, we must face the consequences of our choices. Everything we do affects someone in our life, from our good choices to our bad ones. Someone is always watching us.

"But who do you say that I am?"

I was reminded of consequences in a good way in late 2002 when I was taking a bus from Jerusalem to Ashqelon. Because I was a part-time bus driver at the time, I was really impressed at how the driver handled his bus. He drove it so smoothly that you knew he had the comfort of his passengers in mind. As I got off the bus, I told him as best I could in Hebrew what a good job he had done and that I was a bus driver in America. He thanked me—in English! Well, a few weeks later as I was waiting for a bus in Ashqelon, a young woman approached me and said she was on that bus that day when I complimented the bus driver. She thought it was a nice thing to do and thanked me. I am using this example, not for my glory, but as an example of good choices and their effects. And, admittedly, it is much more gratifying to talk about right choices than wrong choices and their consequences. I have already described the suffering I experienced as the result of the latter; for example, my family and I experienced suffering as a consequence of the sin in my life; my making those bad choices led to broken marriages, children without their father and much more. Eventually that lifestyle (i.e., alcoholism, adultery, worldly success, narcissism) contributed to my depression and resulting suicide attempt.

Second, suffering in our lives may have nothing to do with us but everything to do with the workings of God to reach others through us. When my daughter Melissa was in kindergarten, there was a disadvantaged boy in her class, and her school did not place disadvantaged students in a separate class, which I think most of the parents supported wholeheartedly. It allowed the other students to bring these "special" children along with them, so to speak. And

"But who do you say that I am?"

the love for this particular boy that developed among his classmates was like a magnet, pulling them into the common cause of helping him. It was beautiful to watch this loving interaction among these children. Certainly the love of Christ was displayed in their young lives, and it was felt by us as parents as well.

In John 9, Jesus healed a blind man who was suffering for a greater purpose and not as a consequence of sin. When He was asked if this man had been blind since birth because of his sin or the sin of his parents, Jesus answered, *"Neither this man nor his parents sinned, but that the works of God should be revealed in him"* (John 9:3).

Third, I believe we suffer because from suffering we learn to persevere, and through perseverance we grow, we build character (Romans 5:3–4), and find our Lord and His compassion and mercy. As James said in his epistle, *"Indeed we count them blessed who endure. You have heard of the perseverance of Job and seen the end intended by the Lord—that the Lord is very compassionate and merciful"* (James 5:11).

It was my suffering with depression (also as a consequence of the lifestyle I had chosen) that led to the suicide attempt. But it was my Lord and Savior who patiently waited for me to reach the end of my strength and finally turn to Him (my choice) so He could help me. If we honestly look at our sufferings, we can see the things we have learned from them and the growth in our lives that has resulted from them.

The story of Job is a great example of this kind of suffering, and like every other story in the Bible, it is included for our edification and instruction. Please read it if you haven't already. In it one will see that this righteous man lost everything he possessed, including his children. We learn about integrity when Job would not forsake God, even though he felt he didn't deserve this catastrophe (Job 2: 9-10). We learn from Job about humility when Job was reminded, *"Where were you when I laid the foundations of the earth? Tell Me if you have understanding"* (Job 38:4). And near the end of this great story of "hanging in there," of Job's extraordinary perseverance through suffering, we learn how important it is to put others first because it was then the Lord double-blesses Job. He returns everything Job lost plus *"twice as much as he had before"* *"when he [Job] prayed for his friends"* (Job 42:10).

To bring this point on suffering closer to home: Just before my visit with Julie and Keith, Xavier, who was about four years old at the time, pulled scalding hot water down on himself in an attempt to help his mother prepare a meal. It was one of those times when you see a catastrophe about to happen, but you can't get there quickly enough. Julie just couldn't get to Xavier quickly enough. She rushed him to the hospital and found a burn specialist there, a miracle in itself when you consider the small town they live in. The treatment that was prescribed for Xavier involved bathing him every day to keep the burned area on his chest and chin clean and then applying ointment on the area to prevent infection.

Needless to say, this was all very painful for Xavier. And when I arrived shortly after his accident, I witnessed his screaming when he would yell at his parents, "Why are you doing this to me?" as Julie and Keith would take turns applying this very necessary treatment for him. It was painful to watch, and no amount of reassuring could comfort poor Xavier, who was in terrible pain. It was very difficult for Julie

"But who do you say that I am?"

and Keith and me to watch also, as they had no desire to inflict this pain on their son. But they also knew if they didn't, Xavier could very well develop an infection and even die from his injury. Xavier recovered very quickly, with little noticeable scarring.

Today, Xavier is a very sweet boy who loves the Lord and his parents deeply, knowing from experience that they care for him and his well-being very much. This was confirmed later when Xavier was six years old and approached his mother asking her about Jesus. After confirming that Xavier wanted to receive Jesus into his life, Julie led him in prayer that very same day.

One thing that I have learned for sure from my suffering is that there is a God who loves us very much, so much so that our Father in heaven sent His only Son to die for us and pay the price for our sin that we might live with Him for all eternity. And I believe with my whole heart that our Father doesn't like to watch us suffer any more than Julie and Keith wanted to see their son suffer or that He wanted to see Jesus suffer and die. But He also knows what is needed for our greater good, and as Jesus was raised from the dead, we will be, too, far above the pain and the suffering of this world. Jesus promises us that, *"God will wipe away every tear from their eyes; there shall be no more death, nor sorrow, nor crying. There shall be no more pain, for the former things have passed away"* (Revelation 21:4). And in Isaiah 25:8b–9, God promises, *"And the Lord GOD will wipe away tears from all faces; The rebuke of His people He will take away from all the earth; For the LORD has spoken. And it will be said in that day: 'Behold, this is our God; We have waited for Him, and He will save us. This is the LORD; we have waited for Him;*

"But who do you say that I am?"

We will be glad and rejoice in His salvation." (Taken from "Ransomed: Let the redeemed of the LORD say so..." – Pages 36-40)

As our experiences in trials and suffering impact others it can, in a positive way, draw them to Jesus. The impact on King Nebuchadnezzar through Shadrach, Meshach and Abed-Nego's faith made a profound impression on the king, so much so it brought the king into faith in God.

> *"Then Nebuchadnezzar went near the mouth of the burning fiery furnace and spoke, saying, "Shadrach, Meshach, and Abed-nego, servants of the Most High God, come out, and come here." Then Shadrach, Meshach, and Abed-nego came from the midst of the fire. And the satraps, administrators, governors, and the king's counselors gathered together, and they saw these men on whose bodies the fire had no power; the hair of their head was not singed nor were their garments affected, and the smell of fire was not on them.*
>
> *Nebuchadnezzar spoke, saying, 'Blessed be the God of Shadrach, Meshach, and Abed-nego, who sent His Angel and delivered His servants who trusted in Him, and they have frustrated the king's word, and yielded their bodies, that they should not serve nor worship any god except their own God! Therefore I make a decree that any people, nation, or language which speaks anything amiss against the God of Shadrach, Meshach, and Abed-nego shall be cut in pieces, and their houses shall be made an ash heap; because there is no other God who can deliver like this.' Then the king promoted Shadrach, Meshach, and Abed-nego in the province of Babylon'"* (Daniel 3:26-30).

"But who do you say that I am?"

In whatever the manner Jesus chose to expound about His faithfulness in support of Shadrach, Meshach and Abed-Nego's, in this passage from Daniel to His disciples, is a matter of speculation. I would not be surprised, however, if this story was one in which Jesus did share and explain to His disciples. The reason I believe this is because Jesus has referenced Daniel before and that was when He was teaching on the Great Tribulation (Matthew 24:15 and Mark 13:14; Daniel 11:31 and 12:11).

It is interesting to note that in the Gospels, Jesus is referred to as the "Son of God" 28 times (NKJV). Of those 28 times, 14 or only half, were uttered by believers in Jesus. When one looks at the number of times (87) the "Son of Man" is used to describe Jesus, one can see God's role and focus being the "Suffering Servant" of man while on Earth. After His resurrection His disciples saw Jesus as God, and we to will see Jesus in all His glory upon His triumphant return as King of kings and Lord of lords.

> *"But Jesus kept silent. And the high priest answered and said to Him, 'I put You under oath by the living God: Tell us if You are the Christ, the Son of God!'*
>
> *Jesus said to him, 'It is as you said. Nevertheless, I say to you, hereafter you will see the Son of Man sitting at the right hand of the Power, and coming on the clouds of heaven.'"* (Matthew 26:63-64). Halleluyah!!!

PART II

MESSIANIC PROPHESIES

CHAPTER SEVEN

THE SEED OF GOD

Luke 24:27
And beginning at Moses and all the Prophets,
He expounded to them in all the Scriptures
the things concerning Himself.

C learly we have only touched on a fraction of what
Jesus may have explained about Himself to His disciples during His Resurrection Day as they walked together
on the road to Emmaus. In these last few chapters we will
look specifically at some key prophesies concerning Jesus'
First and Second Comings. We will review three aspects of
these prophesies: 1) The Theme; 2) The Prophecy and 3) The
Fulfillment Status, as currently known at this writing. My
comments are intended to bring some clarity to these beautiful prophecies, but please ask the Holy Spirit to give you
complete understanding in these very important Truths.

"But who do you say that I am?"

1) THEME

Messiah to be seed of the woman

PROPHECY

Genesis 3:15
And I will put enmity Between you and the woman, And between your seed and her Seed; He shall bruise your head, And you shall bruise His heel."

FULFILLMENT

Matthew 1:21
And she will bring forth a Son, and you shall call His name JESUS, for He will save His people from their sins."

Luke 2:21
And when eight days were completed for the circumcision of the Child, His name was called JESUS, the name given by the angel before He was conceived in the womb.

Galatians 4:4-5
But when the fullness of the time had come, God sent forth His Son, born of a woman, born under the law, to redeem those who were under the law, that we might receive the adoption as sons.

COMMENT

The Seed referred to in this prophecy is JESUS. He is our Intercessor now in heaven at the right hand of our Father,

"But who do you say that I am?"

Jesus will forever be between us and the serpent, the devil, until He returns in His glory to rule the world.

"And the God of peace will crush Satan under your feet shortly. The grace of our Lord Jesus Christ be with you. Amen." (Romans 16:20)

2) THEME

Messiah to be seed of Abraham

PROPHECY

Genesis 12:3, 22:18
I will bless those who bless you, And I will curse him who curses you; And in you all the families of the earth shall be blessed."

In your seed all the nations of the earth shall be blessed, because you have obeyed My voice."

FULFILLMENT

Luke 3:23; 3:34
*Now **Jesus Himself** began His ministry at about thirty years of age, being (as was supposed) the son of Joseph, the son of Heli,...the son of Jacob, the son of Isaac, **the son of Abraham**, the son of Terah, the son of Nahor,*

Acts 3:25
You are sons of the prophets, and of the covenant which God made with our fathers, saying to Abraham, 'And in your seed all the families of the earth shall be blessed.'

Galatians 3:16
Now to Abraham and his Seed were the promises made. He does not say, "And to seeds," as of many, but as of one, "And to your Seed," who is Christ.
(Emphasis added)

COMMENT

Again we see the emphasis on the Seed that God will provide to bless and redeem us. As it was from the very beginning of the Bible we see how this Seed was protected by God so that He could come forth and redeem His fallen people. This protection of the Seed started from the birth of Seth, the son of Adam and Eve to replace Able who was slain by his brother Cain.

"For God so loved the world that He gave His only begotten Son (**His Seed**)*, that whoever believes in Him should not perish but have everlasting life."*
(John 3:16-emphasis added)

3) THEME

Messiah to be Lamb of God

PROPHECY

Genesis 22:8
And Abraham said, "My son, God will provide for Himself the lamb for a burnt offering." So the two of them went together.

FULFILLMENT

John 1:29
The next day John saw Jesus coming toward him, and said, "Behold! The Lamb of God who takes away the sin of the world!

John 1:36
And looking at Jesus as He walked, he said, "Behold the Lamb of God!"

John 8:56
Your father Abraham rejoiced to see My day, and he saw it and was glad."

COMMENT

One can only repeat what is said in heaven before the throne of God for all Jesus has done for us; *"Worthy is the Lamb who was slain To receive power and riches and wisdom, And strength and honor and glory and blessing!"* (Revelation 5:12)

4) THEME

Messiah to be of the Tribe of Judah

PROPHECY

Genesis 49:10
The scepter shall not depart from Judah, Nor a lawgiver from between his feet, Until **Shiloh** (Messiah-Strong's #7886, emphasis added) *comes; And to Him shall be the obedience of the people.*

"But who do you say that I am?"

FULFILLMENT

Matthew 1:2
Abraham begot Isaac, Isaac begot Jacob, and Jacob begot Judah and his brothers.

Hebrews 7:14
For it is evident that our Lord arose from Judah, of which tribe Moses spoke nothing concerning priesthood.

Revelation 5:5
But one of the elders said to me, "Do not weep. Behold, the Lion of the tribe of Judah, the Root of David, has prevailed to open the scroll and to loose its seven seals."

COMMENT

In the genealogy of Jesus Christ, listed in Luke 3:23-38, one can see Jesus' direct connection to Judah in verse 3:33; *"the son of Amminadab, the son of Ram, the son of Hezron, the son of Perez, the son of Judah,"*

"And they sang a new song, saying: "You are worthy to take the scroll, And to open its seals; For You were slain, And have redeemed us to God by Your blood Out of every tribe and tongue and people and nation," (Revelation 5:9).

"But who do you say that I am?"

5) THEME

Messiah leads with grace

PROPHECY

Exodus 33:12-13
Then Moses said to the LORD, "See, You say to me, 'Bring up this people.' But You have not let me know whom You will send with me. Yet You have said, 'I know you by name, and you have also found grace in My sight.'

Now therefore, I pray, if I have found grace in Your sight, show me now Your way, that I may know You and that I may find grace in Your sight. And consider that this nation is Your people."

Exodus 23:20
"Behold, I send an Angel before you to keep you in the way and to bring you into the place which I have prepared.

FULFILLMENT

John 1:17
For the law was given through Moses, but grace and truth came through Jesus Christ.

Ephesians 4:7-8
But to each one of us grace was given according to the measure of Christ's gift.

"But who do you say that I am?"

Therefore He says: "When He ascended on high, He led captivity captive, And gave gifts to men" (Ephesians 4:8; Psalm 68:18).

1 Corinthians 2:9
But as it is written: "Eye has not seen, nor ear heard, Nor have entered into the heart of man The things which God has prepared for those who love Him."

COMMENT

What is grace? Grace is unmerited favor or as Webster's Dictionary describes it; "unmerited help". Jesus gives us help, by the Holy Spirit, what the law could not give us. He gave us salvation, the favor of His Grace. The law could not save us. The law points out where we "fall short of the glory of God." However, God's plan brings us out from under the law of sin which the blood of goats and calves could not accomplish. Salvation is ours by just believing in the Son of God. So they said," Believe on the Lord Jesus Christ, and you will be saved, you and your household." (Acts 16:31) Halleluyah!!!

Not with the blood of goats and calves, but with His own blood He entered the Most Holy Place once for all, having obtained eternal redemption.

For if the blood of bulls and goats and the ashes of a heifer, sprinkling the unclean, sanctifies for the purifying of the flesh, how much more shall the blood of Christ, who through the eternal Spirit offered Himself without spot to God, cleanse your conscience from dead works to serve the living God?

And for this reason He is the Mediator of the new covenant, by means of death, for the redemption of the transgressions under the first covenant, that

"But who do you say that I am?"

those who are called may receive the promise of the eternal inheritance. (Hebrews 9:12-15)

6) THEME

Messiah cleanses us and atones for our sins by His blood

PROPHECY

Leviticus 17:11
For the life of the flesh is in the blood, and I have given it to you upon the altar to make atonement for your souls; for it is the blood that makes atonement for the soul.'

FULFILLMENT

Mark 14:24
And He said to them, "This is My blood of the new covenant, which is shed for many.

Romans 3:21-26
*But now the righteousness of God apart from the law is revealed, being witnessed by the Law and the Prophets, even the righteousness of God, through faith in Jesus Christ, to all and on all who believe. For there is no difference; for all have sinned and fall short of the glory of God, being justified freely by His grace through the redemption that is in Christ Jesus, whom God set forth as a propitiation **by His blood**, through faith, to demonstrate His righteousness, because in His forbearance **God had passed over the sins** that were previously committed, to demonstrate at the present time His righteousness,*

"But who do you say that I am?"

that He might be just and the justifier of the one who has faith in Jesus. (Emphasis added)

COMMENT

What is faith and how are we saved through faith alone? Hebrews 11:1 (The Faith Chapter) gives us the perfect definition. *"Now faith is the substance of things hoped for, the evidence of things not seen."*

Faith is the key ingredient in our walk with the Lord Jesus. Having faith in God we:

1. Are saved and are justified in God's eyes through Jesus Christ-Romans 3:21-26; Luke 7:50
2. *"...The just shall live by his faith"*-Habakkuk 2:4
3. Are provided for in all our needs-Matthew 6:30-34
4. Are forgiven and are healed-Matthew 9:2-7; Isaiah 53:5
5. Can move a mountain-Matthew 17:20
6. Are sanctified-Acts 26:18
7. Understand faith and live in it (Faithfulness)-Hebrews 11

7) THEME

Messiah to be seed of Jacob

PROPHECY

Numbers 24:17
"I see Him, but not now; I behold Him, but not near; A Star shall come out of Jacob; A Scepter shall rise out of Israel, And batter the brow of Moab, And destroy all the sons of tumult.

"But who do you say that I am?"

FULFILLMENT

Luke 3:34
the son of Jacob, the son of Isaac, the son of Abraham, the son of Terah, the son of Nahor,

Matthew 1:17
So all the generations from Abraham to David are fourteen generations, from David until the captivity in Babylon are fourteen generations, and from the captivity in Babylon until the Christ are fourteen generations.

Matthew 2:1-2
*Now after Jesus was born in Bethlehem of Judea in the days of Herod the king, behold, wise men from the East came to Jerusalem, saying, "Where is He who has been born King of the Jews? For we have seen **His star** in the East and have come to worship Him."*

1 Corinthians 15:23-26
*But each one in his own order: Christ the firstfruits, afterward those who are Christ's at His coming. Then comes the end, when He delivers the kingdom to God the Father, when He puts an end to all rule and all authority and power. For He must reign till He has put **all enemies under His feet**. The last enemy that will be destroyed is death.* (Emphasis added)

COMMENT

The fulfillment of prophecy predicting Jesus' coming also tells us the importance of the genealogy records in the Bible before His birth. These lineages show to us the faith-

"But who do you say that I am?"

fulness of God who told the devil, after the fall of Adam and Eve into sin, that He (God) would *"put enmity Between you and the woman, and between your seed and her Seed."*

These genealogies also show us how God protected His Seed through all those years prior to Jesus' Coming. At God's perfect time, He planted His Seed in a young Jewish girl who would bring forth the only begotten Son of God. Then through Jesus' sacrifice on the cross He became our Savior, our Messiah, saving us from the penalty of sin and the sin nature we inherited from Adam and Eve. It is, therefore, by no coincidence that we do not see anymore genealogies written in the Bible after Jesus' birth. God's Seed is here! Halleluyah!!!

8) THEME

Messiah to be a prophet like Moses

PROPHECY

Deuteronomy 18:15, 18-19
"The LORD your God will raise up for you a Prophet like me from your midst, from your brethren. Him you shall hear,... I will raise up for them a Prophet like you from among their brethren, and will put My words in His mouth, and He shall speak to them all that I command Him. And it shall be that whoever will not hear My words, which He speaks in My name, I will require it of him.

FULFILLMENT

John 1:45; 6:14; 14:10
Philip found Nathanael and said to him, "We have found Him of whom Moses in the law, and also

86

"But who do you say that I am?"

the prophets, wrote — Jesus of Nazareth, the son of Joseph."

Then those men, when they had seen the sign that Jesus did, said, "This is truly the Prophet who is to come into the world."

Do you not believe that I am in the Father, and the Father in Me? The words that I speak to you I do not speak on My own authority; but the Father who dwells in Me does the works.

COMMENT

There is only one verse in all of the Old Testament where the "Prophet" is mentioned in prophecy. It is in the above verse, Deuteronomy 18:15. There is only one Person who fulfilled that prophecy, Jesus Christ.

Jesus continually gave praise and glory to His Father. Jesus' whole mission on Earth was to do the will of His Father who abided in Him. This must be our primary purpose in life also and we can only fulfill that requirement by abiding in Jesus. Jesus said, *"I am the vine, you are the branches. He who abides in Me, and I in him, bears much fruit; for without Me you can do nothing"* (John 15:5). May God's will be the desire of our hearts.

"For in Him dwells all the fullness of the Godhead bodily; and you are complete in Him, who is the head of all principality and power." (Colossians 2:9-10).

"But who do you say that I am?"

9) THEME

Messiah to be of the seed of David

PROPHECY

2 Samuel 7:8,16
*Now therefore, thus shall you say to My servant David, 'Thus says the **LORD of hosts:** "I took you from the sheepfold, from following the sheep, to be ruler over My people, over Israel...And your house and your kingdom shall be established forever before you. Your throne shall be established forever."'"*
(Emphasis added)

Isaiah 11:10
"And in that day there shall be a Root of Jesse, Who shall stand as a banner to the people; For the Gentiles shall seek Him, And His resting place shall be glorious."

Jeremiah 23:5; 33:15
"Behold, the days are coming," says the LORD, "That I will raise to David a Branch of righteousness; A King shall reign and prosper, And execute judgment and righteousness in the earth.

'In those days and at that time I will cause to grow up to David A Branch of righteousness; He shall execute judgment and righteousness in the earth.

Luke 1:31-33
And behold, you will conceive in your womb and bring forth a Son, and shall call His name JESUS. He will be great, and will be called the Son of the Highest; and the Lord God will give Him the throne

"But who do you say that I am?"

*of His father David. And He will reign over the house
of Jacob forever, and of His kingdom there will be no
end."*

FULFILLMENT

Luke 2:21
*And when eight days were completed for the circum-
cision of the Child, His name was called JESUS, the
name given by the angel before He was conceived in
the womb.*

Matthew 1:17
*So all the generations from Abraham to David are
fourteen generations, from David until the captivity
in Babylon are fourteen generations, and from the
captivity in Babylon until the Christ are fourteen
generations.*

Romans 1:3
*concerning His Son Jesus Christ our Lord, who was
born of the seed of David according to the flesh.*
(Emphasis added)

COMMENT

It is important to know the difference in the genealogies of Jesus as reported in Matthew (1:2-16) and in Luke
(3:23-38). The genealogy in Matthew is from Joseph's
family and is the way lineages were traditionally reported
in Jesus' day, from the father's side (head of the household).
However, the genealogy in Luke is believed to be taken from
Jesus' mother, Mary. Why the two different methods? One
main reason may be that Joseph did not father Jesus. Jesus
was conceived in Mary by the Holy Spirit (Matthew 1:20).

"But who do you say that I am?"

Therefore, the genealogy of Mary's lineage shows Jesus as the Seed of King David, preserving God's plan.

10) THEME

Messiah to be Son of God

PROPHECY

Daniel 3:25
"Look!" he answered, "I see four men loose, walking in the midst of the fire; and they are not hurt, and the form of the fourth is like the Son of God" (Theophany).

Psalms 2:7
"I will declare the decree: The LORD has said to Me, 'You are My Son, Today I have begotten You.

Proverbs 30:4
Who has ascended into heaven, or descended? Who has gathered the wind in His fists? Who has bound the waters in a garment? Who has established all the ends of the earth? What is His name, and what is His Son's name, If you know?

Luke 1:32
He will be great, and will be called the Son of the Highest; and the Lord God will give Him the throne of His father David.

"But who do you say that I am?"

FULFILLMENT

Matt 3:17
And a voice from heaven said, "This is my Son, whom I love; with him I am well pleased."

Matthew 14:31-33
And immediately Jesus stretched out His hand and caught him, and said to him, "O you of little faith, why did you doubt?" And when they got into the boat, the wind ceased. Then those who were in the boat came and worshiped Him, saying, "Truly You are the Son of God."

John 1:48-49
Nathanael said to Him, "How do You know me?" Jesus answered and said to him, "Before Philip called you, when you were under the fig tree, I saw you."
Nathanael answered and said to Him, "Rabbi, You are the Son of God! You are the King of Israel!"

John 6:68-69
But Simon Peter answered Him, "Lord, to whom shall we go? You have the words of eternal life. Also we have come to believe and know that You are the Christ, the Son of the living God."

Luke 22:70
Then they all said, "Are You then the Son of God?" So He said to them, "You rightly say that I am."

Mark 15:37-39
And Jesus cried out with a loud voice, and breathed His last. Then the veil of the temple was torn in two from top to bottom. So when the centurion, who stood

"But who do you say that I am?"

opposite Him, saw that He cried out like this and breathed His last, he said, "Truly this Man was the Son of God!"

COMMENT

Among both non-Christians and some Christians, for that matter the Deity of Christ is the one Truth that is hard for them to grasp (or believe). Then coupled with that is the concept of the Father, Son and Holy Spirit, *"The fullness of the Godhead"* (Colossians 2:9-10); Jesus being One God and Father of us all.

Hopefully, the explanations of Scripture within this book will be a means whereby the Lord will reveal His Truth to those remaining in a state of unbelief.

My personal understanding on the concept of the Godhead and an explanation I have found helpful is to look at the Father, Son and Holy Spirit (One God) relationship in a similar way we see our own families today. For example, a father within a family is also a son to his father, and he is also a husband to his wife. These are three very distinct relationships, but he is still one person. And looking in Scripture we can see God referring to Himself in three very distinct terms, Father, Son and Holy Spirit.

Let us look then at a few examples in the Bible where we see God referring to Himself as Father, Son and the Holy Spirit:

First, God as Father can be found in Deuteronomy 32:6; *"Do you thus deal with the LORD, O foolish and unwise people? Is He not your **Father**, who bought you? Has He not made you and established you?"* We see also in 1 Chronicles 29:10 that, *"Therefore David blessed the LORD before all the assembly; and David said: "Blessed are You, LORD God of Israel, our **Father**, forever and ever."* And finally in Malachi 2:10, we read that the Father is God and our Creator. *"Have*

"But who do you say that I am?"

*we not all one **Father**? Has not **one God** created us? Why do we deal treacherously with one another By profaning the covenant of the fathers?"* In the Old Testament God is referred to as "Father" some 16 times; in the New Testament 260 times.

Second, we can see God as the Son of God, for example, in Psalm 2:7 and 2:12; *"I will declare the decree: The LORD has said to Me, 'You are My **Son**, Today I have begotten You…Kiss the **Son**, lest He be angry, And you perish in the way, When His wrath is kindled but a little. Blessed are all those who put their trust in Him."* But probably the most revealing testimony of God being His Son is His manifestation to the three sons of Israel, Shadrach, Meshach, and Abed-nego, whom King Nebuchadnezzar had thrown into the "fiery furnace" for not worshipping his idol. *"Look!"* *he answered, "I see four men loose, walking in the midst of the fire; and they are not hurt, and the form of the fourth is like the **Son of God**"* (Daniel 3:25). Clearly this is a pre-incarnate manifestation of Jesus Himself as we have read in Chapter Six.

In God as the Holy Spirit we see Him mentioned in the very first verse of the Bible, Genesis 1:1; *"The earth was without form, and void; and darkness was on the face of the deep. And the **Spirit of God** was hovering over the face of the waters."* We can also see here in this verse the "Husband" role of God, as the earth is being prepared in the womb of light and darkness.

This same role of "Husband" was also involved in the conception of Jesus when Joseph was being assured by an angel to take Mary to be his wife even though she was with child, as we see in Matthew 1:20; *"But while he thought about these things, behold, an angel of the Lord appeared to him in a dream, saying, "Joseph, son of David, do not be afraid to take to you Mary your wife, for that which is conceived in her is of the **Holy Spirit**."* And we see in Hosea

93

"But who do you say that I am?"

2:16, God is referring to Himself as one day being reunited again to His people Israel as their Husband. *"And it shall be, in that day," Says the LORD, "That you will call Me 'My Husband, 'And no longer call Me 'My Master.'"*

The Holy Spirit also fulfills the role of our Counselor as we see in Isaiah 11:2 when we are told about Jesus; *"The Spirit of the LORD shall rest upon Him, The Spirit of wisdom and understanding, The Spirit of counsel and might, The Spirit of knowledge and of the fear of the LORD."* As our Counselor, He will teach us the way of God. *"Teach me to do Your will, For You are my God; Your Spirit is good. Lead me in the land of uprightness"* (Psalms 143:10). And Jesus confirms this when He says in Luke 12:12, *"For the Holy Spirit will teach you in that very hour what you ought to say."*

Finally, we find references to our One God in three distinct rolls of the God-Head when Isaiah prophesied the coming of our Messiah, Jesus, our "Prince of Peace;" *"For unto us a Child is born, Unto us a Son is given; And the government will be upon His shoulder. And His name will be called Wonderful, Counselor, Mighty God, Everlasting Father, Prince of Peace"* (Isaiah 9:6-emphasis added).

Halleluyah!!!

CHAPTER EIGHT

MESSIAH'S BIRTH AND MISSION

Isaiah 9:6
For unto us a Child is born,
Unto us a Son is given;
And the government will be upon His shoulder.
And His name will be called
Wonderful, Counselor,
Mighty God, Everlasting Father, Prince of Peace.

11) THEME

Messiah is to be born of a virgin

PROPHECY

Isaiah 7:14
Therefore the Lord Himself will give you a sign:
Behold, the virgin shall conceive and bear a Son, and
shall call His name Immanuel.

"But who do you say that I am?"

FULFILLMENT

Matthew 1:18-25

Now the birth of Jesus Christ was as follows: After His mother Mary was betrothed to Joseph, before they came together, she was found with child of the Holy Spirit. Then Joseph her husband, being a just man, and not wanting to make her a public example, was minded to put her away secretly. But while he thought about these things, behold, an angel of the Lord appeared to him in a dream, saying, "Joseph, son of David, do not be afraid to take to you Mary your wife, for that which is conceived in her is of the Holy Spirit. And she will bring forth a Son, and you shall call His name JESUS, for He will save His people from their sins."

So all this was done that it might be fulfilled which was spoken by the Lord through the prophet, saying: "Behold, the virgin shall be with child, and bear a Son, and they shall call His name Immanuel," which is translated, "God with us."

Then Joseph, being aroused from sleep, did as the angel of the Lord commanded him and took to him his wife, and did not know her till she had brought forth her firstborn Son. And he called His name JESUS.

COMMENT

These passages prompt us to recall the first prophesy from God about the coming of Jesus when He said in Genesis 3:15, *"And I will put enmity Between you and the woman, And between your seed and her Seed; He shall bruise your head, And you shall bruise His heel."*

"But who do you say that I am?"

Let us never forget how faithful God is to His promises and what it cost Him to "ransom" us from the penalty of sin. Halleluyah!!!

12) THEME

Messiah is to be born in Bethlehem

PROPHECY

Micah 5:2
"But you, Bethlehem Ephrathah, Though you are little among the thousands of Judah, Yet out of you shall come forth to Me The one to be Ruler in Israel, Whose goings forth are from of old, From everlasting."

FULFILLMENT

Luke 2:4-6
*Joseph also went up from Galilee, out of the city of Nazareth, into Judea, to the **city of David**, which is called **Bethlehem**, because he was of the house and lineage of David, to be registered with Mary, his betrothed wife, who was with child. So it was, that while they were there, the days were completed for her to be delivered.*

Luke 2:11
*For there is born to you this day in the **city of David** a **Savior**, who is **Christ the Lord**.*

Matthew 2:1-2
*Now after **Jesus was born in Bethlehem** of Judea in the days of Herod the king, behold, wise men from*

97

"But who do you say that I am?"

the East came to Jerusalem, saying, "Where is He who has been born King of the Jews? For we have seen His star in the East and have come to worship Him." (Emphasis added)

COMMENT

Bethlehem is mentioned 51 times in the Bible; 42 times in the Old Testament and 9 times in the New Testament. Bethlehem comes from the Hebrew word, "Ephrath," which means "fruitfulness" and from the root word, "parah," meaning to "bear fruit" (Strong's concordance Nos. 672 and 6509). Rachel, Isaac's wife, was buried in Bethlehem. King David, Israel's greatest king, came from Bethlehem. Most importantly, Jesus, the King of kings and the Lord of lords was born to us in Bethlehem to become the "ransom for many" (the Firstfruits of God our Father).

Halleluyah!!!

13) THEME

Messiah's Mission

PROPHECY

Genesis 3:15
And I will put enmity Between you and the woman, And between your seed and her Seed; He shall bruise your head, And you shall bruise His heel."

Psalms 14:7
Oh, that the salvation of Israel would come out of Zion! When the LORD brings back the captivity of His people, Let Jacob rejoice and Israel be glad.

"But who do you say that I am?"

Isaiah 59:16
He saw that there was no man, And wondered that there was no intercessor; Therefore His own arm brought salvation for Him; And His own righteousness, it sustained Him.

Isaiah 62:11
Indeed the LORD has proclaimed To the end of the world: "Say to the daughter of Zion, 'Surely your salvation is coming; Behold, His reward is with Him, And His work before Him.'"

Isaiah 45:17
But Israel shall be saved by the LORD With an everlasting salvation; You shall not be ashamed or disgraced Forever and ever.

Isaiah 49:5-6
"And now the LORD says, Who formed Me from the womb to be His Servant, To bring Jacob back to Him, So that Israel is gathered to Him (For I shall be glorious in the eyes of the LORD, And My God shall be My strength), Indeed He says, 'It is too small a thing that You should be My Servant To raise up the tribes of Jacob, And to restore the preserved ones of Israel; I will also give You as a light to the Gentiles, That You should be My salvation to the ends of the earth.'"

Isaiah 61:1-2a
"The Spirit of the Lord GOD is upon Me, Because the LORD has anointed Me To preach good tidings to the poor; He has sent Me to heal the brokenhearted, To proclaim liberty to the captives, And the opening

"But who do you say that I am?"

*of the prison to those who are bound; To proclaim
the acceptable year of the LORD,*

FULFILLMENT

Matthew 15:24
*But He (Jesus) answered and said, "I was not sent
except to the lost sheep of the house of Israel."*

Luke 19:9-10
*And Jesus said to him, "Today salvation has come
to this house, because he also is a son of Abraham;
for the Son of Man has come to seek and to save that
which was lost."*

Luke 4:16-21
*So He (Jesus) came to Nazareth, where He had
been brought up. And as His custom was, He went
into the synagogue on the Sabbath day, and stood up
to read.*

*And He was handed the book of the prophet
Isaiah. And when He had opened the book, He found
the place where it was written: "The Spirit of the
LORD is upon Me, Because He has anointed Me To
preach the gospel to the poor; He has sent Me to
heal the brokenhearted, To proclaim liberty to the
captives And recovery of sight to the blind, To set
at liberty those who are oppressed; To proclaim the
acceptable year of the LORD." Then He closed the
book, and gave it back to the attendant and sat down.
And the eyes of all who were in the synagogue were
fixed on Him.*

*And He began to say to them, "Today this
Scripture is fulfilled in your hearing."*

"But who do you say that I am?"

Luke 2:25-32
And behold, there was a man in Jerusalem whose name was Simeon, and this man was just and devout, waiting for the Consolation of Israel, and the Holy Spirit was upon him. And it had been revealed to him by the Holy Spirit that he would not see death before he had seen the Lord's Christ. So he came by the Spirit into the temple. And when the parents brought in the Child Jesus, to do for Him according to the custom of the law, he took Him up in his arms and blessed God and said: "Lord, now You are letting Your servant depart in peace, According to Your word; For my eyes have seen Your salvation Which You have prepared before the face of all peoples, A light to bring revelation to the Gentiles, And the glory of Your people Israel."

Acts 26:22-23
Therefore, having obtained help from God, to this day I stand, witnessing both to small and great, saying no other things than those which the prophets and Moses said would come — that the Christ would suffer, that He would be the first to rise from the dead, and would proclaim light to the Jewish people and to the Gentiles.

Hebrews 2:14-18
Inasmuch then as the children have partaken of flesh and blood, He Himself likewise shared in the same, that through death He might destroy him who had the power of death, that is, the devil, and release those who through fear of death were all their lifetime subject to bondage. For indeed He does not give aid to angels, but He does give aid to the seed of Abraham. Therefore, in all things He had to be made

like His brethren, that He might be a merciful and faithful High Priest in things pertaining to God, to make propitiation for the sins of the people.
For in that He Himself has suffered, being tempted, He is able to aid those who are tempted. (Emphasis added)

COMMENT

Much has been written about Jesus, our Savior, by many people whose lives have been forever changed by their personal and saving relationship with Him. In fact, as John said in John 21:25, *"And there are also many other things that Jesus did, which if they were written one by one, I suppose that even the world itself could not contain the books that would be written. Amen."*

In my case, I was in the "pit of despair" and approaching death when a simple cry, "God, forgive me" changed my whole life by bringing me into a personal relationship with our Father, through Jesus Christ. I should have died that morning, but God heard my cry and He honored His promise as written in Joel 2:32 and Romans 10:13, *'"For "whoever calls on the name of the LORD shall be saved."'*

In God's mercy, my physical body was also saved, but my spiritual and eternal salvation is a gift of immeasurable worth. I am reconciled to the Father, sealed by the Holy Spirit, protected and loved forever and ever by the One, Jesus Christ. His mission was *"To preach the gospel to the poor; He has sent Me to heal the brokenhearted, To proclaim liberty to the captives And recovery of sight to the blind, To set at liberty those who are oppressed; To proclaim the acceptable year of the LORD."* Halleluyah!!!

"But who do you say that I am?"

14) THEME

Messiah will heal many and perform miracles

PROPHECY

Isaiah 35:4-6
Say to those who are fearful-hearted, "Be strong, do not fear! Behold, your God will come with vengeance, With the recompense of God; He will come and save you." Then the eyes of the blind shall be opened, And the ears of the deaf shall be unstopped. Then the lame shall leap like a deer, And the tongue of the dumb sing. For waters shall burst forth in the wilderness, And streams in the desert.

FULFILLMENT

Matthew 15:30-31
Then great multitudes came to Him, having with them the lame, blind, mute, maimed, and many others; and they laid them down at Jesus' feet, and He healed them. So the multitude marveled when they saw the mute speaking, the maimed made whole, the lame walking, and the blind seeing; and they glorified the God of Israel.

John 11:43-44
Now when He had said these things, He cried with a loud voice, "Lazarus, come forth!" And he who had died came out bound hand and foot with grave-clothes, and his face was wrapped with a cloth. Jesus said to them, "Loose him, and let him go."

"But who do you say that I am?"

Matthew 11:4-6
Jesus answered and said to them, "Go and tell John the things which you hear and see: The blind see and the lame walk; the lepers are cleansed and the deaf hear; the dead are raised up and the poor have the gospel preached to them. And blessed is he who is not offended because of Me."

John 11:47
Then the chief priests and the Pharisees gathered a council and said, "What shall we do? For this Man works many signs.

COMMENT

I would hope all of us would have a story of how the Lord Jesus has healed maladies within us or in our families' lives especially when we have prayed for their healing.

I remember getting word that both my daughter and mother-in-law had been diagnosed with cancer within a few days of each other. After receiving this terrible news, I sent out a request for prayer for their healing among my friends. Our prayers were answered within a few months when both received healing. The doctor who treated my mother-in-law proclaimed to her it was a miracle! Halleluyah!!!

It is possible you may be reading these accounts and wondering why your prayers for healing or other petitions haven't materialized as you had expected, for yourself or for another. It is important to remember that the Lord's ways are not always our ways. Be assured when your prayers are made in belief for healing, for example, healing does take place. The healing may not have manifested physically, as we know it, but the Lord is concerned also for our spiritual healing. We should always be thankful to the Lord for the

"But who do you say that I am?"

healing, whether we see it or not, for we have His promise...
"By His stripes we are healed" (Isaiah 53:5).

CHAPTER NINE

THE MESSIAH AND HIS MIRACLES

Matthew 11:4-5
And when John had heard in prison about the works of Christ, he sent two of his disciples and said to Him, "Are You the Coming one, or do we look for another?"
Jesus answered and said to them, "Go and tell John the things which you hear and see:
The blind see and the lame walk; the lepers are cleansed and the deaf hear;
the dead are raised up and the poor have the gospel preached to them.

During Jesus' ministry on earth He performed many miracles. The focus of this chapter is to look at five of Jesus' miracles of healing that answer prophesies about them and specifically who would perform them.

We can see from the above verses that Jesus was pointing out to John (the Baptist) specific miracles which He had done to answer John's question on whether He (Jesus) was *"the Coming one, or do we look for another?"* One might

"But who do you say that I am?"

ask, why did Jesus mention these five particular miracles? And from those five miracles, why would John then recognize Jesus to be the Messiah? After all, some of those same miracles were performed by prophets of the Old Testament and before Jesus' birth.

In answering John, Jesus was reminding him of what Isaiah prophesied about the Messiah and His miracles when he said in Isaiah 35:4-6, *"Say to those who are fearful-hearted, 'Be strong, do not fear!* **Behold, your God will come** *with vengeance, With the recompense of God;* **He will come and save you.***' Then the* **eyes of the blind shall be opened**, *And* **the ears of the deaf shall be unstopped**. *Then* **the lame shall leap like a deer**, *And the* **tongue of the dumb sing**. *For waters shall burst forth in the wilderness, And streams in the desert'"* (emphasis added). And again in Isaiah 61:1, *"The* **Spirit of the Lord GOD is upon Me**, *Because the* **LORD** *has* **anointed Me** *To preach good tidings to the poor; He has sent* **Me to heal the brokenhearted**, *To* **proclaim liberty** *to the captives, And the* **opening of the prison** *to those who are* **bound***;"* (emphasis added).

Now let's take a closer look at each of Jesus' divine healings. The first miracle Jesus points out to John is that *"the blind see"*. This is very important because there are no recorded healings of the blind in the Old Testament. Further more, God said to Moses in Exodus 4:11, *"...Who has made man's mouth? Or who makes the mute, the deaf, the seeing, or the blind? Have not I, the LORD?"* Our Creator makes it absolutely clear Who makes the blind and Who makes the seeing, only our LORD GOD.

Jesus further makes this point when he healed the man blind since birth in John 9:1-7. When Jesus' disciples asked Jesus if the man was made blind because of his sins or the sins of his parents Jesus answered and said, *"Neither this man nor his parents sinned, but that the works of God should be revealed in him" (John 9:3)*. The rest of this chapter

108

"But who do you say that I am?"

deals with the unbelief (blindness) of the religious leaders of that day in refusing to accept Jesus for Who He really is, even after seeing with their own eyes the cured blind man. This healed man now summed it up perfectly when he said, *"Since the world began it has been unheard of that anyone opened the eyes of one who was born blind. If this Man were not from God, He could do nothing" (John 9:32-33).* This "Man" is Jesus, the Messiah, the Holy One of Israel and God incarnate who came to heal **all** our infirmities and open our spiritual eyes to behold Him.

The second miracle Jesus mentioned was that *"the lame walk"*. Again, here is another miracle that has no precedence in the Old Testament. Why would Jesus put emphasis on healing the lame? Because, I believe, He wanted to show us we need Him if we are to walk in righteousness. Remember when Jesus healed the paralytic and before he healed him physically He forgave his sins (Matthew 9:2)? In the spiritual sense lameness could be looked at as not walking in obedience to God, hence Jesus forgave his sins freeing him to now walk upright according to the will of God.

The third miracle and "sign" Jesus performed was the healing of the lepers. Now before we look closer at this miracle let us remember that lepers were healed in the Old Testament time. Miriam, Moses' sister was healed (even Moses himself was healed when God used it as a sign to show Moses the power that God would display through him in order to convince Pharaoh to "let (His) people go"-Exodus 4:6-7). Then there was Naaman, the king of Syria's servant, who was cured through Elisha the prophet's intercession (2 Kings 5:1-14). But all these healings were done by God through His servants.

Now we have Jesus, God in the flesh, performing these healings. However, of all the healings of leprosy recorded in the Old Testament none were ever presented to the priest for verification until Jesus' healing of the leper in Matthew

"But who do you say that I am?"

8:2-4. Notice also in this passage that the leper came to Jesus and *"worshipped Him, saying, "Lord, if You are willing, You can make me clean"'* (8:2). Only God is worshipped, therefore, this leper knew he was petitioning the Almighty. And, Jesus, recognizing his faith said, *"I am willing; be cleansed"* (8:3). Then *"Jesus said to him, 'See that you tell no one; but go your way, show yourself to the priest, and offer the gift that Moses commanded, as a testimony to them"'* (8:4). The cleansing here was not only from leprosy but sin itself.

The fourth sign Jesus mentions as a witness to His claim to be Israel's Messiah is that *"the deaf hear"*. In Mark 9:14-29 we see a wonderful story of God's power compared to men. This is the story of the young boy who was brought to Jesus' disciples to cast out a deaf and dumb spirit. They could not, so the boys father pleaded with Jesus to *"have compassion on us..."*. Jesus rebuked them for their lack of faith (Mark 9:19) and then Jesus said, *"Bring him to me."*

Prior to this miracle three of Jesus' disciples had been on the Mountain of Transfiguration and witnessed Jesus in all His glory with Moses and Elijah. Our lack of faith (deafness-"faith comes by hearing..."-Romans 10:17) gets in the way of what we believe and can prevent us from helping others who have never heard of their Messiah. However, Jesus can cure that illness today as He did back then if we but turn to Him to "have compassion on us".

The fifth miracle Jesus pointed out to John was the raising of the dead. Now in 1 Kings 17:20-22 we can read where Elijah prayed for a widow's son who had died and God restored him to life. Also we can see in 2 Kings 4:32-35 where Elisha interceded for another boy who had died and God restored him too. But those miracles were accomplished by petitioning God to intercede and bring them back to life. However, Jesus didn't need to petition God because He is God and "the resurrection and the life" (John 11:25). Jesus commanded and life was restored at once.

"But who do you say that I am?"

We can see this in Jesus' raising of the widow's son (Luke 7:12-15); the raising of Jairus' daughter, a ruler of a synagogue (Mark 5:22-24; 35-42) and the raising of Lazarus (John 11:1-44). Lazarus' resurrection is an especially powerful display of God's omnipotence because Lazarus had been dead for four days. This is important to note because it was a Jewish custom in those days for someone to stand watch by the tomb for three days in case a person was not really dead and so they could release them from the sealed tomb. With Lazarus being in the tomb for four days there was no question that he was dead. That is why Martha said to Jesus when He asked for the stone to be rolled away from the tomb, *"Lord, by this time there is a stench, for he has been dead four days"* (John 11:39). Jesus was about to make it very clear Who it was that gives life. He later commanded, *"Lazarus, come forth! And he who had died came out **bound** hand and foot with graveclothes, and his face was wrapped with a cloth. Jesus said to them, 'Loose him, and let him go"'* (John 11:43-44-emphasis added).

Jesus' miracles of raising the dead, from a spiritual standpoint, tell us that no matter how dead in sin we are, He can give us new life when we have "godly sorrow" in our heart and believe in Him. We can see this promise in 2 Corinthians 5:17; *"Therefore, if anyone is in Christ, he is a new creation; old things have passed away; behold, all things have become new."*

Isaiah prophesied that the Messiah to come would perform these miracles, curing not only their physical ailments but also their spiritual diseases that were preventing their salvation. Jesus fulfilled those prophecies in a very powerful way establishing to John the Baptist (and to us) that, not only was He the promised Messiah, but also, The Great "I AM", God Himself.

And, finally, one of the ways Jesus proclaimed His Deity (God Himself) was showing us His power over His creation.

"But who do you say that I am?"

Therefore, if we look at this passage from Psalm 107 we will see one of the ways God is sovereign over all heaven and earth:

*"Those who go down to the sea in ships, Who do business on great waters, They see the works of the LORD, And His wonders in the deep. For **He commands and raises the stormy wind**, Which lifts up the waves of the sea. They mount up to the heavens, They go down again to the depths; **Their soul melts because of trouble**. They reel to and fro, and stagger like a drunken man, And are at their wits' end. **Then they cry out to the LORD** in their trouble, **And He brings them out of their distresses. He calms the storm, So that its waves are still**."* Psalms (107:23-29-emphasis added)

Now let us look at this passage from Mark 4 and see Jesus manifesting His Deity by showing us the Sovereignty of God over the wind and the waves:

*"Now when they had left the multitude, they took Him (Jesus) along in the boat as He was. And other little boats were also with Him. And **a great windstorm arose**, and the **waves beat into the boat**, so that it was already filling. But He was in the stern, asleep on a pillow. And they awoke Him and said to Him, **'Teacher, do You not care that we are perishing?'**

Then He (Jesus) arose and rebuked the wind, and said to the sea, 'Peace, be still!'' And the wind ceased and there was a great calm. But He said to them, 'Why are you so fearful? How is it that you have no faith?''* '
(Mark 4:36-40-emphasis added)

"But who do you say that I am?"

It is amazing to me, when we look at what Jesus did while He was here on earth. How His words and deeds declare the praise and glory of our Wonderful God, Who loves us so much that He would die to atone for our sins, so that we may live with Him for all eternity. Halleluyah!!!

And there are also many other things that Jesus did, which if they were written one by one, I suppose that even the world itself could not contain the books that would be written. Amen (John 21:25).

CHAPTER TEN

MESSIAH'S PASSION AND TRIUMPH

ᚲᚱᚢ ᚱᚲᚢ

Zechariah 9:9
"Rejoice greatly, O daughter of Zion! Shout,
O daughter of Jerusalem! Behold, your King is
coming to you;
He is just and having salvation, Lowly and riding
on a donkey,
A colt, the foal of a donkey.

15) THEME

Messiah will enter Jerusalem on a donkey

PROPHECY

Genesis 22:3; 7-8
So Abraham rose early in the morning and saddled his donkey, and took two of his young men with him, and Isaac his son; and he split the wood for the burnt offering, and arose and went to the place of which God had told him.

115

But Isaac spoke to Abraham his father and said, "My father!" And he said, "Here I am, my son." Then he said, "Look, the fire and the wood, but where is the lamb for a burnt offering?" And Abraham said, "My son, God will provide for Himself the lamb for a burnt offering." So the two of them went together.

Zechariah 9:9
"Rejoice greatly, O daughter of Zion! Shout, O daughter of Jerusalem! Behold, your King is coming to you; He is just and having salvation, Lowly and riding on a donkey, A colt, the foal of a donkey.

FULFILLMENT

Matthew 21:1-9
Now when they drew near Jerusalem, and came to Bethphage, at the Mount of Olives, then Jesus sent two disciples, saying to them, "Go into the village opposite you, and immediately you will find a donkey tied, and a colt with her. Loose them and bring them to Me. And if anyone says anything to you, you shall say, 'The Lord has need of them,' and immediately he will send them."

All this was done that it might be fulfilled which was spoken by the prophet, saying: "Tell the daughter of Zion, 'Behold, your King is coming to you, Lowly, and sitting on a donkey, A colt, the foal of a donkey.'" So the disciples went and did as Jesus commanded them. They brought the donkey and the colt, laid their clothes on them, and set Him on them.

And a very great multitude spread their clothes on the road; others cut down branches from the trees and spread them on the road. Then the multitudes who went before and those who followed cried out,

"But who do you say that I am?"

saying: "Hosanna to the Son of David! 'Blessed is He who comes in the name of the LORD! 'Hosanna in the highest!"

COMMENT

In Chapter Two, we recognized the relationship between the accounts of Abraham offering his son Isaac as a sacrificial offering to God recorded in Genesis 22 and the future event when Jesus rode triumphantly into Jerusalem on a donkey in preparation for the sacrifice that would seal our salvation as recorded in Matthew 21.

The use of a donkey, a beast of burden, is significant in its symbolism in the supporting role to Isaac's obedience to the will of his father for Abraham's sake and Jesus' obedience to the will of His Father for the salvation of all mankind. These two events were the only recorded times in the Bible a donkey was used in carrying the burden for sacrifice.

16) THEME

Messiah to be betrayed by a friend

PROPHECY

Psalms 41:9
Even my own familiar friend in whom I trusted, Who ate my bread, Has lifted up his heel against me.

Zechariah 11:12-13
Then I said to them, "If it is agreeable to you, give me my wages; and if not, refrain." So they weighed out for my wages thirty pieces of silver. And the LORD said to me, "Throw it to the potter" — that princely price they set on me. So I took the thirty pieces of

117

silver and threw them into the house of the LORD for the potter.

FULFILLMENT

John 13:18,21
"I do not speak concerning all of you. I know whom I have chosen; but that the Scripture may be fulfilled, 'He who eats bread with Me has lifted up his heel against Me.'... When Jesus had said these things, He was troubled in spirit, and testified and said, "Most assuredly, I say to you, one of you will betray Me."

Matthew 26:14-16,25
Then one of the twelve, called Judas Iscariot, went to the chief priests and said, "What are you willing to give me if I deliver Him to you?" And they counted out to him thirty pieces of silver. So from that time he sought opportunity to betray Him.

Then Judas, who was betraying Him, answered and said, "Rabbi, is it I?" He said to him, "You have said it."

Matthew 27:3-7
Then Judas, His betrayer, seeing that He had been condemned, was remorseful and brought back the thirty pieces of silver to the chief priests and elders, saying, "I have sinned by betraying innocent blood." And they said, "What is that to us? You see to it!" Then he threw down the pieces of silver in the temple and departed, and went and hanged himself. But the chief priests took the silver pieces and said, "It is not lawful to put them into the treasury, because they are the price of blood." And they consulted together and

"But who do you say that I am?"

bought with them the potter's field, to bury strangers
in.

COMMENT

We might say, "How could Judas do that? After all he
was with Jesus when he heard Him speak and witnessed His
many miracles. What would posses a man to fall as low as to
betray His Messiah?

If we look at this situation honestly we can see we have
all betrayed Jesus in one way or another. Any time we have
selfishly chosen anything available to us in this world instead
of our obedience to Jesus, isn't this a betrayal of our Lord?

Let me relate a personal example. On any given Sunday,
instead of going to church and worshipping our Lord, haven't
we decided to stay home to watch some sport's playoff on
TV? Then later felt guilty about it? The hope for us is that we
can change our attitudes by submitting ourselves to Jesus, as
a faithful servant, and let the Power of the Holy Spirit work
in us *"to will and to do for His good pleasure"* (Philippians
2:13).

17) THEME

Messiah to be forsaken by His disciples

PROPHECY

Zechariah 13:7
*"Awake, O sword, against My Shepherd, Against
the Man who is My Companion," Says the LORD
of hosts. "Strike the Shepherd, And the sheep will be
scattered; Then I will turn My hand against the little
ones.*

"But who do you say that I am?"

FULFILLMENT

Matthew 26:31
Then Jesus said to them, "All of you will be made to stumble because of Me this night, for it is written: 'I will strike the Shepherd, And the sheep of the flock will be scattered.'

Matthew 26:56
But all this was done that the Scriptures of the prophets might be fulfilled." Then all the disciples forsook Him and fled.

COMMENT

Today, in this fallen world, many people have fled the calling of the Lord. Admittedly, not everyone is called to pastor a church, for example, but this is not the only way of what is meant by being one of Jesus' disciples. Instead, as is stated in Ephesians 4:11-12, Jesus has given *"...some to be apostles, some prophets, some evangelists, and some pastors and teachers, for the equipping of the saints for the work of ministry, for the edifying of the body of Christ,"* (Ephesians 4:11-12).

Our duty is to answer His call whether it is in the workplace, mission field, and local community or in our church. There are more souls brought to salvation through Jesus outside the church building then inside of it. If we waited inside a church to be used by the Lord to bring others to the Lord then hardly any one would be saved and encouraged. This is precisely the reason it is so important to answer His call, no matter where God has placed us, to be used by Him to point anyone and everyone to Jesus for salvation and encouragement. No one should be left behind!

"But who do you say that I am?"

"The Lord is not slack concerning His promise, as some count slackness, but is longsuffering toward us, not willing that any should perish but that all should come to repentance." (2 Peter 3:9).

18) THEME

Messiah will be smitten and scourged

PROPHECY

Isaiah 50:6
I gave My back to those who struck Me, And My cheeks to those who plucked out the beard; I did not hide My face from shame and spitting.

Isaiah 52:14
Just as many were astonished at you, So His visage was marred more than any man, And His form more than the sons of men;

Isaiah 53:4-5
Surely He has borne our griefs And carried our sorrows; Yet we esteemed Him stricken, Smitten by God, and afflicted. But He was wounded for our transgressions, He was bruised for our iniquities; The chastisement for our peace was upon Him, And by His stripes we are healed.

FULFILLMENT

Matthew 26:67; 27:30
Then they spat in His face and beat Him; and others struck Him with the palms of their hands,...Then they

121

"But who do you say that I am?"

spat on Him, and took the reed and struck Him on the head.

Mark 15:15
So Pilate, wanting to gratify the crowd, released Barabbas to them; and he delivered Jesus, after he had scourged Him, to be crucified.

COMMENT

The film, "The Passion of the Christ," has been a subject of controversy, even within the Christian community. At the top of the list of the controversy is that the scenes of the beatings of Christ before His crucifixion were brutally vivid. For me it portrayed the enormous amount of suffering it cost God to purchase our salvation for us. It was not just the physical torture He endured, but those scenes from the movie gave me a sense of the mental, emotional and spiritual suffering He took upon Himself to "save a wretch like me." It is beyond my earthbound comprehension to fully grasp and appreciate what our Lord God and Savior did for us to be saved. I will continue to thank my Lord, Jesus Christ, throughout all eternity. And by the power of the Holy Spirit, I will learn to live a life in the likeness of Him.

19) THEME

Messiah's crucifixion

PROPHECY

Genesis 22:6,8,9
So Abraham took the wood of the burnt offering and laid it on Isaac his son; and he took the fire in his hand, and a knife, and the two of them went

"But who do you say that I am?"

*together...And Abraham said, "My son, God will provide for Himself the lamb for a burnt offering." So the two of them went together...Then they came to the place of which God had told him. And Abraham built an altar there and placed the wood in order; and he **bound Isaac** his son and laid him on the altar, **upon the wood**...Then Abraham lifted his eyes and looked, and there behind him was a **ram caught** in a **thicket by its horns**. So Abraham went and took the ram, and **offered it** up for a burnt offering **instead of his son**.*

Psalms 22:8,16,18,3
"He trusted in the LORD, let Him rescue Him; Let Him deliver Him, since He delights in Him!"...For dogs have surrounded Me; The congregation of the wicked has enclosed Me. They pierced My hands and My feet;... They divide My garments among them, And for My clothing they cast lots...They will come and declare His righteousness to a people who will be born, That He has done this.

Psalms 69:21
They also gave me gall for my food, And for my thirst they gave me vinegar to drink.

Isaiah 49:16
*See, I have **inscribed you** on the **palms of My hands**; Your walls are continually before Me.*

Isaiah 53
Who has believed our report? And to whom has the arm of the LORD been revealed? For He shall grow up before Him as a tender plant, And as a root out of dry ground. He has no form or comeliness; And

123

*when we see Him, There is no beauty that we should desire Him. He is despised and rejected by men, A Man of sorrows and acquainted with grief. And we hid, as it were, our faces from Him; He was despised, and we did not esteem Him. Surely He has borne our griefs And carried our sorrows; Yet we esteemed Him stricken, Smitten by God, and afflicted. **But He was wounded for our transgressions**, He was **bruised for our iniquities**; The chastisement for our peace was upon Him, **And by His stripes we are healed**. All we like sheep have gone astray; We have turned, every one, to his own way; And the LORD has laid on Him the iniquity of us all. He was oppressed and He was afflicted,*

*Yet He opened not His mouth; He was led as a lamb to the slaughter, And as a sheep before its shearers is silent, So He opened not His mouth. He was taken from prison and from judgment, And who will declare His generation? For **He was cut off from the land of the living; For the transgressions of My people He was stricken**. And they made His grave with the wicked — But with the rich at His death, Because He had done no violence, Nor was any deceit in His mouth. Yet it pleased the LORD to bruise Him; He has put Him to grief. When You make **His soul an offering for sin**, He shall see His seed, He shall prolong His days, And the pleasure of the LORD shall prosper in His hand. **He shall see the labor of His soul, and be satisfied**. By His knowledge **My righteous Servant shall justify many**, For He shall bear their iniquities. Therefore I will divide Him a portion with the great, And He shall divide the spoil with the strong, Because He poured out His soul unto death, And He was numbered with* *the transgressors, And **He bore the sin of many, And made intercession for the transgressors**.*

Daniel 9:26
*"And after the sixty-two weeks **Messiah shall be cut off**, but not for Himself; And the people of the prince who is to come Shall destroy the city and the sanctuary. The end of it shall be with a flood, And till the end of the war desolations are determined.* (Emphasis added)

FULFILLMENT

Matthew 27:34-50
they gave Him sour wine mingled with gall to drink. But when He had tasted it, He would not drink. Then they crucified Him, and divided His garments, casting lots, that it might be fulfilled which was spoken by the prophet: "They divided My garments among them, And for My clothing they cast lots." Sitting down, they kept watch over Him there. And they put up over His head the accusation written against Him: THIS IS JESUS THE KING OF THE JEWS. Then two robbers were crucified with Him, one on the right and another on the left. And those who passed by blasphemed Him, wagging their heads and saying, "You who destroy the temple and build it in three days, save Yourself! If You are the Son of God, come down from the cross." Likewise the chief priests also, mocking with the scribes and elders, said, "He saved others; Himself He cannot save. If He is the King of Israel, let Him now come down from the cross, and we will believe Him.

He trusted in God; let Him deliver Him now if He will have Him; for He said, 'I am the Son of God.'"

"But who do you say that I am?"

Even the robbers who were crucified with Him reviled Him with the same thing.

Now from the sixth hour until the Ninth hour there was darkness over all the land.

And about the Ninth hour Jesus cried out with a loud voice, saying, "Eli, Eli, lama sabachthani?" that is, "My God, My God, why have You forsaken Me?" Some of those who stood there, when they heard that, said, "This Man is calling for Elijah!" Immediately one of them ran and took a sponge, filled it with sour wine and put it on a reed, and offered it to Him to drink. The rest said, "Let Him alone; let us see if Elijah will come to save Him." And Jesus cried out again with a loud voice, and yielded up His spirit.

John 19:28-30; 38-42

After this, Jesus, knowing that all things were now accomplished, that the Scripture might be fulfilled, said, "I thirst!" Now a vessel full of sour wine was sitting there; and they filled a sponge with sour wine, put it on hyssop, and put it to His mouth. So when Jesus had received the sour wine, He said, "It is finished!" And bowing His head, He gave up His spirit.

After this, Joseph of Arimathea, being a disciple of Jesus, but secretly, for fear of the Jews, asked Pilate that he might take away the body of Jesus; and Pilate gave him permission. So he came and took the body of Jesus. And Nicodemus, who at first came to Jesus by night, also came, bringing a mixture of myrrh and aloes, about a hundred pounds. Then they took the body of Jesus, and bound it in strips of linen with the spices, as the custom of the Jews is to bury. Now in the place where He was crucified there was a garden, and in the garden a new tomb in which no one had

"But who do you say that I am?"

yet been laid. So there they laid Jesus, because of the Jews' Preparation Day, for the tomb was nearby.

COMMENT

There are seven key declarations that Jesus made on the cross before *"He gave up His spirit."* These are written about in "Ransomed: Let the redeemed of the LORD say so..." and I will share them with you now. His words not only summarize why Christ died for us, but they provide the example for us to live by:

1) *"Father, forgive them, for they do not know what they do"* (Luke 23:34). I must always forgive those who I believe have hurt me.
2) *"Assuredly, I say to you, today you will be with me in Paradise" (Luke 23:43).* After I seek forgiveness and ask Jesus into my life, I will see Jesus in Paradise someday. (see also Luke 11:4)
3) *"Woman, behold your son!...Behold your mother!"* (John 19:26-27). I should always consider family and others before myself.
4) *"My God, My God, why have you forsaken me?"* (Mark 15:34). It is all right to tell God my true feelings.
5) *"I thirst!"* (John 19:28). After others, I can certainly petition God for my needs and He wants me to.
6) *"It is finished!"* (John 19:30). My mission on earth is complete when God says it is complete.
7) *"Father, into Your hands I commit My spirit"* (Luke 23:46). In all things may God's will be the desire of my heart.

The key to the process of transformation—a continuing process until we are with the Lord—is to accept Jesus as

"But who do you say that I am?"

Lord of our lives. And then ask for (Luke 11:13) and allow the Holy Spirit to work in our lives *"to will and to do* for *His good pleasure"* (Philippians 2:13). Because God has given us a free will, He is looking for our agreement in making His will the *"desire of our heart."* That is saying yes to God in everything. As I have found, without letting this supernatural Power act on our behalf, it is impossible for us to change and be separated from those things that are sinful and hurtful to God, our family, our friends, and others whom God puts in our lives. For Jesus said, *"But the Helper, the Holy Spirit, whom the Father will send in My name, He will teach you all things, and bring to your remembrance all things that I said to you"* (John 14:26). As we allow, this process will continue for the rest of our lives here on earth because, as Jesus says, *"I am the vine, you are the branches. He who abides in Me, and I in him, bears much fruit; for without Me you can do nothing"* (John 15:5). And as Paul went on to explain in his epistle, *"Being confident of this very thing, that He who has begun a good work in you will complete it until the day of Jesus Christ'"* (Philippians 1:6). Praise God!!!" (pages 50-51)

CHAPTER ELEVEN

MESSIAH'S GLORY

᠊ᡱᠣ᠍᠊ᡲᡉ᠍᠊

Luke 24:26
Ought not the Christ to have suffered these things and to enter into His glory?"

20) THEME

Messiah to be raised from the dead

PROPHECY

Job 19:25-27
For I know that my Redeemer lives, And He shall stand at last on the earth;
And after my skin is destroyed, this I know, That in my flesh I shall see God,
Whom I shall see for myself, And my eyes shall behold, and not another. How my heart yearns within me!

Psalms 16:10
For You will not leave my soul in Sheol, Nor will You allow Your Holy one to see corruption.

"But who do you say that I am?"

FULFILLMENT

Matthew 28:5-6
But the angel answered and said to the women, "Do not be afraid, for I know that you seek Jesus who was crucified. He is not here; for He is risen, as He said. Come, see the place where the Lord lay.

Mark 16:14
Later He appeared to the eleven as they sat at the table; and He rebuked their unbelief and hardness of heart, because they did not believe those who had seen Him after He had risen.

Luke 24:33-35
So they rose up that very hour and returned to Jerusalem, and found the eleven and those who were with them gathered together, saying, "The Lord is risen indeed, and has appeared to Simon!" And they told about the things that had happened on the road, and how He was known to them in the breaking of bread.

John 20:11-17
But Mary stood outside by the tomb weeping, and as she wept she stooped down and looked into the tomb. And she saw two angels in white sitting, one at the head and the other at the feet, where the body of Jesus had lain. Then they said to her, "Woman, why are you weeping?" She said to them, "Because they have taken away my Lord, and I do not know where they have laid Him." Now when she had said this, she turned around and saw Jesus standing there, and did not know that it was Jesus. Jesus said to

"But who do you say that I am?"

her, "Woman, why are you weeping? Whom are you seeking?" She, supposing Him to be the gardener, said to Him, "Sir, if You have carried Him away, tell me where You have laid Him, and I will take Him away." Jesus said to her, "Mary!" She turned and said to Him, "Rabboni!" (which is to say, Teacher). Jesus said to her, "Do not cling to Me, for I have not yet ascended to My Father; but go to My brethren and say to them, 'I am ascending to My Father and your Father, and to My God and your God.'"

Acts 1:11
who also said, "Men of Galilee, why do you stand gazing up into heaven? This same Jesus, who was taken up from you into heaven, will so come in like manner as you saw Him go into heaven."

Acts 2:23-32
Him, being delivered by the determined purpose and foreknowledge of God, you have taken by lawless hands, have crucified, and put to death; whom God raised up, having loosed the pains of death, because it was not possible that He should be held by it.

For David says concerning Him: 'I foresaw the LORD always before my face, For He is at my right hand, that I may not be shaken. Therefore my heart rejoiced, and my tongue was glad; Moreover my flesh also will rest in hope. For You will not leave my soul in Hades, Nor will You allow Your Holy one to see corruption.

You have made known to me the ways of life; You will make me full of joy in Your presence.'

"Men and brethren, let me speak freely to you of the patriarch David, that he is both dead and buried, and his tomb is with us to this day. Therefore, being

a prophet, and knowing that God had sworn with an oath to him that of the fruit of his body, according to the flesh, He would raise up the Christ to sit on his throne, he, foreseeing this, spoke concerning the resurrection of the Christ, that His soul was not left in Hades, nor did His flesh see corruption. This Jesus God has raised up, of which we are all witnesses.

Acts 10:40-41; 13:22-24,35-37

Him God raised up on the third day, and showed Him openly, not to all the people, but to witnesses chosen before by God, even to us who ate and drank with Him after He arose from the dead.

And when He had removed him, He raised up for them David as king, to whom also He gave testimony and said, 'I have found David the son of Jesse, a man after My own heart, who will do all My will.' From this man's seed, according to the promise, God raised up for Israel a Savior — Jesus — after John had first preached, before His coming, the baptism of repentance to all the people of Israel.

Therefore He also says in another Psalm: 'You will not allow Your Holy one to see corruption.' "For David, after he had served his own generation by the will of God, fell asleep, was buried with his fathers, and saw corruption; but He whom God raised up saw no corruption.

Romans 6:4-5,9

Therefore we were buried with Him through baptism into death, that just as Christ was raised from the dead by the glory of the Father, even so we also should walk in newness of life. For if we have been united together in the likeness of His death, certainly we also shall be in the likeness of His resurrection,...

"But who do you say that I am?"

knowing that Christ, having been raised from the dead, dies no more. Death no longer has dominion over Him.

1 Corinthians 15:3-8
For I delivered to you first of all that which I also received: that Christ died for our sins according to the Scriptures, and that He was buried, and that He rose again the third day according to the Scriptures, and that He was seen by Cephas, then by the twelve. After that He was seen by over five hundred brethren at once, of whom the greater part remain to the present, but some have fallen asleep. After that He was seen by James, then by all the apostles. Then last of all He was seen by me also, as by one born out of due time.

2 Timothy 2:8
Remember that Jesus Christ, of the seed of David, was raised from the dead according to my gospel,

COMMENT

A few years ago I had the privilege and honor of visiting the Garden Tomb near Jerusalem where Jesus is thought to have been buried after His crucifixion. While sitting there in the tomb, contemplating my sins that had placed my Savior in this cavern, I experienced the overwhelming sense of the emptiness within that tomb. As I got up to leave, I felt an assurance that I could leave all my sins and guilt behind me; that I should go forward and not look back upon those dark days again.

When I exited Jesus' tomb it felt as though a heavy load had been taken off my shoulders. My spirit felt uplifted far beyond explanation. Then, almost immediately, a sign on

"But who do you say that I am?"

the podium where sermons are preached caught my eye. On it was written, "He is Risen!" Therefore, because of Jesus' Resurrection, we can know for certain; "O Death, where is your sting? O Hades, where is your victory?" (1 Corinthians 15:55).

Please also know that on the very day when we have given our life to Jesus Christ, our sins are forgiven. We can also rejoice because our sins have been atoned for by our Lord and Savior, Who died for us and rose from the dead, so that we may live with Him forever. We are a "new creation."

"Therefore, if anyone is in Christ, he is a new creation; old things have passed away; behold, all things have become new" (2 Corinthians 5:17).

Halleluyah!

21) THEME

Messiah's final victory over death

PROPHECY

Job 19:25-27
For I know that my Redeemer lives, And He shall stand at last on the earth;
And after my skin is destroyed, this I know, That in my flesh I shall see God*, Whom I shall see for myself, And my eyes shall behold, and not another. How my heart yearns within me!*

Psalms 18:5,19
The sorrows of Sheol surrounded me; The snares of death confronted me.

"But who do you say that I am?"

He also brought me out into a broad place; He delivered me because He delighted in me.

Psalms 56:13
For You have delivered my soul from death. Have You not kept my feet from falling, That I may walk before God In the light of the living?

Psalms 116:8-9
*For You have **delivered my soul from death**, My eyes from tears, And my feet from falling. **I will walk before the LORD In the land of the living**.*

Proverbs 12:28
In the way of righteousness is life, And in its pathway there is no death.

Isaiah 25:8-9
***He will swallow up death forever**, And the Lord GOD will wipe away tears from all faces; The rebuke of His people He will take away from all the earth; For the LORD has spoken. And it will be said in that day: "Behold, this is our God; We have waited for Him, and He will save us. This is the LORD; We have waited for Him; **We will be glad and rejoice in His salvation**."*

Hosea 13:14
***"I will ransom them from the power of the grave; I will redeem them from death**. O Death, I will be your plagues! **O Grave, I will be your destruction!** Pity is hidden from My eyes."* (Emphasis added)

"But who do you say that I am?"

FULFILLMENT

Matthew 16:28
Assuredly, I say to you, there are some standing here who shall not taste death till they see the Son of Man coming in His kingdom."

Matthew 20:18-19
"Behold, we are going up to Jerusalem, and the Son of Man will be betrayed to the chief priests and to the scribes; and they will condemn Him to death, and deliver Him to the Gentiles to mock and to scourge and to crucify. And the third day He will rise again."

John 11:11; 43-44
These things He said, and after that He said to them, "Our friend Lazarus sleeps, but I go that I may wake him up."

Now when He had said these things, He cried with a loud voice, "Lazarus, come forth!" And he who had died came out bound hand and foot with graveclothes, and his face was wrapped with a cloth. Jesus said to them, "Loose him, and let him go."

1 Corinthians 15:54-57
*So when this corruptible has put on incorruption, and this mortal has put on immortality, then shall be brought to pass the saying that is written: "**Death is swallowed up in victory**."*

*"**O Death, where is your sting**? O Hades, where is your victory?" The sting of death is sin, and the strength of sin is the law. **But thanks be to God, who gives us the victory through our Lord Jesus Christ**.*

"But who do you say that I am?"

Revelation 7:17
for the Lamb who is in the midst of the throne will shepherd them and lead them to living fountains of waters. And God will wipe away every tear from their eyes."

Again in Revelation 21:4 God says; *"And God will wipe away every tear from their eyes; there shall be **no more death**, nor sorrow, nor crying. There shall be no more pain, for the former things have passed away."* (Emphasis added)

COMMENT

Jesus' victory over death for all of us is so very real and vivid in my body, soul and spirit today.

It is important here that I elaborate more on my testimony that I shared with you earlier. Jesus' victory over death also gave me victory over death in a very powerful way.

There had been a time in my life when I felt there was nothing and no one to live for. It was then I made a serious attempt at ending my life. But our Lord was and is faithful and merciful because He heard my cry for His forgiveness just before the bullet entered my head. As it says in Joel 2:32 and Romans 10:13, *"For 'whoever calls on the name of the LORD shall be saved.'"* I should not be here, but by the grace of God I was miraculously saved from the jaws of death. Not only physical death, but what could have been separation from God, for all eternity.

Yes, Jesus' victory over death is for all who want to believe in Him. This gives me hope for those loved ones in my life who have died. There are some who I am not sure if they received Jesus into their hearts before they passed on. But I know what can happen in those very few seconds that separate us from this life and the next, because I know what

"But who do you say that I am?"

the Lord Jesus had done for me in those few seconds I had remaining. Praise God!!!

22) THEME

Messiah's Great Commission

PROPHECY

1 Chronicles 16:23
Sing to the LORD, all the earth; Proclaim the good news (the gospel) *of His salvation from day to day.*

Psalms 96:2
Sing to the LORD, bless His name; Proclaim the good news of His salvation from day to day.

Proverbs 25:25
As cold water to a weary soul, So is good news from a far country.

Isaiah 52:7
How beautiful upon the mountains Are the feet of him who brings good news, Who proclaims peace, Who brings glad tidings of good things, Who proclaims salvation, Who says to Zion, "Your God reigns!" (Emphasis added)

FULFILLMENT

Matthew 28:18-20
And Jesus came and spoke to them, saying, "All authority has been given to Me in heaven and on earth. Go therefore and make disciples of all the nations, baptizing them in the name of the Father

"But who do you say that I am?"

and of the Son and of the Holy Spirit, teaching them to observe all things that I have commanded you; and lo, I am with you always, even to the end of the age." Amen.

Mark 16:15
And He said to them, "Go into all the world and preach the gospel ("good news") *to every creature.* (Emphasis added)

COMMENT

The word "gospel" came from the Hebrew and Greek words meaning "good news" or "glad tidings." How we spread His "Good News" is comprised of more than what we say. It is also what we think and what we do for the Lord. We should constantly look for those situations where He will provide the opportunity for us to share *"a reason for the hope that is in you, with meekness and fear"* (1 Peter 3:15).

One of the most powerful tools the Lord has given to us to fulfill His "Great Commission" is by the words of our personal testimony. This became very clear to me when I spoke to a congregation in a small church in Kimberley, South Africa. Later, after my testimony, a woman approached me to ask if I would pray for her mother. She said her mother was heavily under the influence of alcohol. They had brought her to this church that day with the hope she could be helped. They did not know what else they could do for her.

As I started to pray for this dear woman, to loose her from her dependence on liquor, her tears started to flow. The Holy Spirit had touched her heart in a mighty and powerful way. When I finished praying for her, I started to walk away, but the Holy Spirit prompted me to go back and ask her if she would like to invite Jesus into her life. I then returned and asked this woman, whom the Holy Spirit had made her

"But who do you say that I am?"

heart ready, if she would like to receive Jesus into her life. She replied eagerly that she did, and that day our LORD GOD brought another soul, who had been perishing, into His Kingdom. Halleluyah!

Through these experiences the Holy Spirit continues to show me how He works through us, sometimes in spite of ourselves. All He wants is a willing vessel. *"For it is God who works in you both to will and to do for His good pleasure"* (Philippians 2:13).

23) THEME

Messiah ascends to heaven

PROPHECY

Psalms 68:18
You have ascended on high, You have led captivity captive; You have received gifts among men, Even from the rebellious, That the LORD God might dwell there.

Proverbs 30:4
Who has ascended into heaven, *or descended? Who has gathered the wind in His fists? Who has bound the waters in a garment? Who has established all the ends of the earth? What is His name, and* ***what is His Son's name, If you know?***

Isaiah 59:16
He saw that there was no man, And wondered that there was no intercessor; Therefore His own arm brought salvation for Him; And His own righteousness, it sustained Him. (Emphasis added)

"But who do you say that I am?"

FULFILLMENT

Ephesians 4:7-8
But to each one of us grace was given according to the measure of Christ's gift.
*Therefore He says: "When **He ascended on high**, He led captivity captive, And gave gifts to men."*

Luke 24:51-53
*Now it came to pass, while He blessed them, that He was parted from them and **carried up into heaven**. And they worshiped Him, and returned to Jerusalem with great joy, and were continually in the temple praising and blessing God. Amen.*

Acts 1:9-11
*Now when He had spoken these things, while they watched, **He was taken up**, and a cloud received Him out of their sight. And while they looked steadfastly toward heaven as He went up, behold, two men stood by them in white apparel, who also said, "Men of Galilee, why do you stand gazing up into heaven? **This same Jesus, who was taken up from you into heaven, will so come in like manner as you saw Him go into heaven."***

Timothy 3:16
*And without controversy great is the mystery of godliness: God was manifested in the flesh, Justified in the Spirit, Seen by angels, Preached among the Gentiles, Believed on in the world, **Received up in glory**.*

Hebrews 9:24-28
For Christ has not entered the holy places made with hands, which are copies of the true, but into heaven

"But who do you say that I am?"

*itself, now **to appear in the presence of God for us**; not that He should offer Himself often, as the high priest enters the Most Holy Place every year with blood of another — He then would have had to suffer often since the foundation of the world; but now, once at the end of the ages, He has appeared to put away sin by the sacrifice of Himself. And as it is appointed for men to die once, but after this the judgment, so Christ was offered once to bear the sins of many. To those who eagerly wait for Him He will appear a second time, apart from sin, for salvation.*

Romans 8:34
*Who is he who condemns? It is Christ who died, and furthermore is also risen, who is **even at the right hand of God**, who also makes intercession for us.*

John 14:2
*In My Father's house are many mansions; if it were not so, I would have told you. **I go to prepare a place for you.*** (Emphasis added)

COMMENT

In the last two verses above we see that Jesus ascended into heaven to be our Intercessor before the Father and to prepare a place for us. What a comfort to know that! First, we know now that Jesus will intercede in our behalf throughout all of our trials, tribulations and failures while we are on this Earth. And, second, to prepare our home with Jesus and our Father.

What is this place in heaven Jesus is preparing for us? It is hard for me to grasp, especially after all that Jesus has done for me. He freely gave to me from the cup of salvation, as well as to all others who believe in Him. What could

"But who do you say that I am?"

possibly be that something more He must do for us? Wasn't Jesus' sacrifice on the cross for the atonement for our sins enough? When one couples that with the statement in the Bible that says, *"Eye has not seen, nor ear heard, Nor have entered into the heart of man The things which God has prepared for those who love Him"* (1 Corinthians 2:9), one can only be amazed and look forward with joyful anticipation to what is in store for all who believe in our Lord Jesus Christ.

Fortunately, we do get a glimpse of what is being prepared for us from what is written in the Bible. In fact, God tells us in 1 Corinthians 2:10, *"But God has revealed them to us through His Spirit. For the Spirit searches all things, yes, the deep things of God."* Part of what is revealed can be seen in the book of Revelation. When reading chapters 21 and 22 of Revelation we can possibly start to imagine what this wonderful "Place" is like that Jesus is preparing for us.

First, as St. John describes for us, *"Then I, John, saw the holy city, New Jerusalem, coming down out of heaven from God, prepared as a bride adorned for her husband"* (Revelation 21:2). Then in verse 4 he says the most incredible thing; *"And God will wipe away every tear from their eyes; there shall be no more death, nor sorrow, nor crying. There shall be no more pain, for the former things have passed away."*

God will wipe away our tears in this wonderful place! The concept that the Almighty will comfort me, after the way I have failed Him in this life is beyond my capability to grasp. "Thank You, Jesus! You died for me and cleansed me from all sin. I know when I go to stand before our Father in heaven He will only see Your righteousness and not my filthy rags." "...I can only imagine...," as the famous song goes from "Mercy Me." What a beautiful place Jesus is preparing for us! Halleluyah!!!

"But who do you say that I am?"

Next, Jesus describes who will be in this place He has prepared for us and who will not be in this place when He said,

"It is done! I am the Alpha and the Omega, the Beginning and the End. I will give of the fountain of the water of life freely to him who thirsts. He who overcomes shall inherit all things, and I will be his God and he shall be My son.

But the cowardly, unbelieving, abominable, murderers, sexually immoral, sorcerers, idolaters, and all liars shall have their part in the lake which burns with fire and brimstone, which is the second death" (Revelation 21:6-8).

Now, below John describes for us, in greater detail, what our Dear Lord Jesus is preparing for those who "overcome."

"And he carried me away in the Spirit to a great and high mountain, and showed me the great city, the holy Jerusalem, descending out of heaven from God, having the glory of God. Her light was like a most precious stone, like a jasper stone, clear as crystal. Also she had a great and high wall with twelve gates, and twelve angels at the gates, and names written on them, which are the names of the twelve tribes of the children of Israel: three gates on the east, three gates on the north, three gates on the south, and three gates on the west.

Now the wall of the city had twelve foundations, and on them were the names of the twelve apostles of the Lamb. And he who talked with me had a gold reed to measure the city, its gates, and its wall.

144

"But who do you say that I am?"

The city is laid out as a square; its length is as great as its breadth. And he measured the city with the reed: twelve thousand furlongs. Its length, breadth, and height are equal. Then he measured its wall: one hundred and forty-four cubits, according to the measure of a man, that is, of an angel. The construction of its wall was of jasper; and the city was pure gold, like clear glass. The foundations of the wall of the city were adorned with all kinds of precious stones: the first foundation was jasper, the second sapphire, the third chalcedony, the fourth emerald, the fifth sardonyx, the sixth sardius, the seventh chrysolite, the Eighth beryl, the Ninth topaz, the tenth chrysoprase, the eleventh jacinth, and the twelfth amethyst.

The twelve gates were twelve pearls: each individual gate was of one pearl. And the street of the city was pure gold, like transparent glass. But I saw no temple in it, for the Lord God Almighty and the Lamb are its temple. The city had no need of the sun or of the moon to shine in it, for the glory of God illuminated it. The Lamb is its light. And the nations of those who are saved shall walk in its light, and the kings of the earth bring their glory and honor into it. Its gates shall not be shut at all by day (there shall be no night there). And they shall bring the glory and the honor of the nations into it. But there shall by no means enter it anything that defiles, or causes an abomination or a lie, but only those who are written in the Lamb's Book of Life" (Revelation 21:10-27).

My prayer is that we all have godly sorrow in our hearts, because *"godly sorrow produces repentance leading to salvation..."* (2 Corinthians 7:10). Once saved our name is written in the "Lamb's Book of Life" and we become a

"But who do you say that I am?"

citizen of this beautiful place our Lord Jesus is preparing for us. And as Hebrews 9:28 tells us; we are to "eagerly wait for Him". The Greek word for "wait" in that verse means, according to Strong's Greek Dictionary; "to expect fully". In other words, it is not a question of "if" we will be with Jesus in this wonderful "place" He is preparing for us, but "when". Halleluyah!!!

24) THEME

Messiah to be at the right hand of God

PROPHECY

Exodus 15:6
"Your right hand, O LORD, has become glorious in power; Your right hand, O LORD, has dashed the enemy in pieces.

Psalms 16:11; 17:7; 20:6; 110:1; 139:10
You will show me the path of life; In Your presence is fullness of joy; At Your right hand are pleasures forevermore.

Show Your marvelous lovingkindness by Your right hand, O You who save those who trust in You From those who rise up against them.

Now I know that the LORD saves His anointed; He will answer him from His holy heaven With the saving strength of His right hand.

The LORD said to my Lord, "Sit at My right hand, Till I make Your enemies Your footstool."

Even there Your hand shall lead me, And Your right hand shall hold me.

"But who do you say that I am?"

Isaiah 41:10
Fear not, for I am with you; Be not dismayed, for I am your God. I will strengthen you, Yes, I will help you, I will uphold you with My righteous right hand.'

FULFILLMENT

Matthew 26:64
Jesus said to him, "It is as you said. Nevertheless, I say to you, hereafter you will see the Son of Man sitting at the right hand of the Power, and coming on the clouds of heaven."

Hebrews 1:1-3
God, who at various times and in various ways spoke in time past to the fathers by the prophets, has in these last days spoken to us by His Son, whom He has appointed heir of all things, through whom also He made the worlds; who being the brightness of His glory and the express image of His person, and upholding all things by the word of His power, when He had by Himself purged our sins, sat down at the right hand of the Majesty on high,

COMMENT

It is interesting to me to see that the "right hand" of God is referenced both in the Old and New Testaments of the Bible. As we know, the importance of those verses was manifested in the Person of Jesus Christ.

"But who do you say that I am?"

25) THEME

Messiah, the Arm of God

PROPHECY

Psalms 98:1
Oh, sing to the LORD a new song! For He has done marvelous things; His right hand and His holy arm have gained Him the victory.

Isaiah 59:16
He saw that there was no man, And wondered that there was no intercessor; Therefore His own arm brought salvation for Him; And His own righteousness, it sustained Him.

Isaiah 53:1
Who has believed our report? And to whom has the arm of the LORD been revealed?

FULFILLMENT

John 12:37-38
But although He had done so many signs before them, they did not believe in Him, that the word of Isaiah the prophet might be fulfilled, which he spoke: "Lord, who has believed our report? And to whom has the arm of the LORD been revealed?"

COMMENT

Under Jesus' strength we can "move mountains." This is pictured so clearly for us when we look at His death and

"But who do you say that I am?"

resurrection. And, with that same Power of God working in our lives, "who can be against us?"

This has become very clear to me as our Lord Jesus took me from depression and attempted suicide right up to the receiving of the gift of His salvation. In removing doubt from Moses the LORD spoke to him in Numbers 11:23 saying, *"Has the LORD's arm been shortened? Now you shall see whether what I say will happen to you or not."*

God is always here for each one of us. Reach up now and take hold of Jesus' Arm and His Righteous Right Hand now.

26) THEME

Messiah's Second Coming

PROPHECY

Job 19:25
For I know that my Redeemer lives, And He shall stand at last on the earth;

Isaiah 59:20
"The Redeemer will come to Zion, And to those who turn from transgression in Jacob," Says the LORD.

Daniel 7:13-14
"I was watching in the night visions, And behold, one like the Son of Man, Coming with the clouds of heaven! He came to the Ancient of Days, And they brought Him near before Him. Then to Him was given dominion and glory and a kingdom, That all peoples, nations, and languages should serve Him. His dominion is an everlasting dominion, Which

shall not pass away, And His kingdom the one Which shall not be destroyed.

Acts 1:11
...″Men of Galilee, why do you stand gazing up into heaven? This same Jesus, who was taken up from you into heaven, will so come in like manner as you saw Him go into heaven.″

Romans 11:25-27
For I do not desire, brethren, that you should be ignorant of this mystery, lest you should be wise in your own opinion, that blindness in part has happened to Israel until the fullness of the Gentiles has come in. And so all Israel will be saved, as it is written: "The Deliverer will come out of Zion, And He will turn away ungodliness from Jacob; For this is My covenant with them, When I take away their sins."

Matthew 16:27; 24:30-31
For the Son of Man will come in the glory of His Father with His angels, and then He will reward each according to his works.

Then the sign of the Son of Man will appear in heaven, and then all the tribes of the earth will mourn, and they will see the Son of Man coming on the clouds of heaven with power and great glory. And He will send His angels with a great sound of a trumpet, and they will gather together His elect from the four winds, from one end of heaven to the other.

Mark 8:38; 14:62
For whoever is ashamed of Me and My words in this adulterous and sinful generation, of him the Son

"But who do you say that I am?"

of Man also will be ashamed when He comes in the glory of His Father with the holy angels."

Jesus said, "I am. And you will see the Son of Man sitting at the right hand of the Power, and coming with the clouds of heaven."

Luke 17:24-25
For as the lightning that flashes out of one part under heaven shines to the other part under heaven, so also the Son of Man will be in His day. But first He must suffer many things and be rejected by this generation.

John 14:18
I will not leave you orphans; I will come to you.

1 Thessalonians 4:16-18
For the Lord Himself will descend from heaven with a shout, with the voice of an archangel, and with the trumpet of God. And the dead in Christ will rise first. Then we who are alive and remain shall be caught up together with them in the clouds to meet the Lord in the air. And thus we shall always be with the Lord. Therefore comfort one another with these words.

Revelation 1:7
Behold, He is coming with clouds, and every eye will see Him, even they who pierced Him. And all the tribes of the earth will mourn because of Him. Even so, Amen.

Revelation 22:12
"And behold, I am coming quickly, and My reward is with Me, to give to every one according to his work.

Revelation 22:20
He who testifies to these things says, "Surely I am coming quickly." Amen. Even so, come, Lord Jesus!

Matthew 23:39
"for I say to you, you shall see Me no more till you say, 'Blessed is He who comes in the name of the LORD!'"

FULFILLMENT

Waiting (in faith) on the LORD

Matthew 24:36
"But of that day and hour no one knows, not even the angels of heaven, but My Father only.

COMMENT

These are wonderful promises of God, to say the least. My words do not seem adequate, nor will they ever be adequate enough to add anything to what God has promised us. In fact, I had thought about not commenting here and just let these chapters end with that beautiful promise of the return of our Messiah Jesus. Then I ran across a note I had written and placed in my Bible titled, "Reflections on Certainty" and under this title was a reference to Psalm 139:17-18. I believe these verses can help us reflect on the personal relationship we have with God, knowing Jesus has made certain our relationship will last, forever! Halleluyah!

How precious also are Your thoughts to me, O God! How great is the sum of them! If I should count them, they would be more in number than the sand; When I awake, I am still with You (Psalms 139:17-18).

"But who do you say that I am?"

We have now seen our Lord and His plan revealed to us through His word. Now we need to put His plan into action as we allow Jesus to join us along that road to "Emmaus". Also, we must, as Paul counsels us in Philippians 2:12-13;

"Therefore, my beloved, as you have always obeyed, not as in my presence only, but now much more in my absence, work out your own salvation with fear and trembling; for it is God who works in you both to will and to do for His good pleasure".

CHAPTER TWELVE

REVELATION

~❧ ❧~

Luke 24:16
But their eyes were restrained,
so that they did not know Him.

"They did not know Him." One can only wonder why these two disciples of Jesus walking on the road to Emmaus didn't recognize Jesus when He joined them on their journey that glorious Resurrection Day (Luke 24:13-35). One of His disciples on that road that day was Cleopas, Mary (the mother of Jesus) sister's husband (John 19:25). Even Mary Magdalene who was one of the first of His followers to see Jesus after His resurrection and the one whom Jesus had cast out "seven demons" (Mark 16:9) didn't recognize Him (John 20:14). Why?

Certainly those who were close to Jesus should have known Him. After all they were with Him for 3 1/2 years. They heard Him teach, they saw His miracles and yet they didn't recognize Him. Could it have been their unbelief because of His crucifixion and seeing Him die an agonizing death, then laid in a sealed tomb, thereby rationalizing that He was just like the prophets of old that had been killed before Him? Even walking this Resurrection Day on the road

155

"But who do you say that I am?"

to Emmaus with His two disciples and explaining about who He (Jesus) is through the Scriptures (The Old Testament), they still did not realize who He really was.

Some two thousand years later many still do not know who Jesus is. It certainly isn't because we don't have churches with wonderful worship services and Bible study groups or any lack of published work about Jesus, for that matter. Could it be some or all of these factors that are the reasons "why" many do not know Jesus today? The answer to knowing Jesus can be seen, I believe, in Luke 24:29, *"But they constrained Him, saying, 'Abide with us, for it is toward evening, and the day is far spent.' And **He went in to stay with them.'"***

We can see from this verse that once Jesus' disciples **invited Him** in to **"Abide with (them)"** He came in *"...then their eyes were opened and they knew Him;"* (Luke 24:31a-emphasis added). In other words, when we **invite Jesus** into our hearts and lives to **abide with us,** then we too will know Him. We will also realize from the Scriptures that Jesus is more than a prophet but our Great "I Am"; God Himself, our "Savior", and "Messiah". That is because, just as Cleopas' and his friend's eyes were opened to the wonderful revelation of Jesus in their lives when they invited Him in, all who invite Jesus into their lives will also say *"Did not our heart burn within us while **He talked with us** on the road, and while **He opened the Scriptures to us?"*** (Luke 24:32-emphasis added).

Therefore, we must let Jesus open our eyes to know Him more fully, whether it be our first time or a closer and more intimate relationship with God that we are seeking. Jesus wants us to experience His love more deeply, and to see His glory, for He has said in Revelation 3:20; *"Behold, I stand at the door and knock. If anyone hears My voice and opens the door, I will come in to him and dine with him, and he with Me."*

"But who do you say that I am?"

Maybe you have never opened the door of your heart to Jesus to let Him into your life. Or maybe your door has been closed to Him because you wanted to walk a way without Him. In either case, we can invite Jesus into our lives again or for the first time by this simple prayer that I also included in my book, "Ransomed: Let the redeemed of the LORD say so...';

"Dear Holy Father, I know I am a sinner and cannot save myself. Please forgive me of my sins. I believe Jesus is my Lord and Savior and that He died for me, paying the penalty for my sins, and that You raised Him from the dead that I may live with You forever. I want Jesus as the Lord of my life so that as Your Holy Spirit lives through me, I will please You as Jesus did. Thank You, Dear Father. I love and praise You. In Jesus' Mighty and Wonderful Name, Amen."

May the door to our hearts come off its hinges so that when Jesus asks us, *"But who do you say that I am?"*, we can answer as confidently as Peter did in Matthew 16:16; *"You are the Christ, the Son of the living God"*. One might also want to add; and I look forward to being with you for all eternity. Halleluyah!!!

Be Blessed in His Love and Shalom!!

ABOUT THE AUTHOR

William Stewart Whittemore is a blessed father
and grandfather. Stewart is a Navy Veteran.
He currently holds an Advanced Diploma in Lay
Biblical Counseling. He appreciates the opportunity to
speak on depression and suicide to encourage others.
Stewart also has written and published "Ransomed:
Let the redeemed of the LORD say so...".

The author may be reached through Xulon Press
or at:
Email - stewart33@earthlink.net

Be Blessed!

CPSIA information can be obtained
at www.ICGtesting.com
Printed in the USA
BVHW071032110419
545224BV00002B/210/P